ALL ABOUT:

COPY EDITING

55 EASY STEPS TO IMPROVE YOUR NOVEL

-K.J.HERITAGE-

Copyright © K.J.Heritage 2020

ALL ABOUT: *COPYWRITING*
55 Easy Steps To Improve Your Novel

Published 2017 by *Sygasm*

All rights reserved

Cover design: *K.J.Heritage*

www.mostlywriting.co.uk

Sygasm

ISBN-9798653266492

For all the riters...

Reviews for *All About Copyediting*

"Very valuable and strongly recommended. Probably not a substitute for a real copy-editor but it comes close. I would apply these rules first and then send your writing off to the editor."

"An extremely useful guide for editing manuscripts, written as a set of editing tips. Some of them I already knew, but the book shed new light on their importance, some were new to me, and I was glad to be made aware of them."

"An excellent little guide that works great as a checklist for polishing your novel. Succinct with just enough examples to get the point across, this book not only tells you how to edit your manuscript, but why you should do it."

"K.J.Heritage makes copy editing easy!"

CONTENTS

Why you need a book about copy-editing 7

INTRODUCTION
Before we start 13
SECTION ONE
Adverbs, adjectives & only 27
SECTION TWO
Overused words 43
SECTION THREE
What is more boring than watching paint dry? 75
SECTION FOUR
Italics, quotations & capitalisation 95
SECTION FIVE
Speech 121
SECTION SIX
Tricky words 137
SECTION SEVEN
Word pairs & homophones 163
SECTION EIGHT
Initial conjunctions & 'ings' 179
SUMMARY
EDIT 55 185

FULL GLOSSARY OF EDITS 187

Why You Need a Book About Copyediting

We are living in a new publishing age. The way books are bought, sold and printed has radically changed. The reason? The move towards self-publishing.

Independent authors can now publish their own novels when they want, how they want, and with a cover they are happy with. Indeed, independent publishing provides many new and exciting opportunities for authors.

To become successful independent authors, we must write and publish as professionally as we can. With that in mind, I created this guide. *All About Copywriting* will not tell you how to self-publish, how to get cool covers, or how to market your publications, but it will explain, in a series of fifty-five edits, how to prepare your manuscript for publication or for submitting to your editor or beta-readers

When you publish as an author, be it on an electronic device such as the Kindle or as a printed novel through Createspace or other print-on-demand services, readers are evaluating your writing by using Free First Chapter, etc. With so many novels competing against one another, you need all the tools you can get to convert interest into a buy…

Welcome to the world of copyediting - the revision, correction and adaptation of a piece of writing for publication. An edit is the singular name given to an individual edit or group of edits in the process of copyediting. By working through this guide, you will apply each of the fifty-five edits to your novel.

These copy-edits include:
- Redundant adjectives & overuse of adverbs
- Over thirty overused words & phrases such as *that, it, up/down, was/were, had, even, got, etc.*
- Overuse of exclamations and the ellipsis
- Proper use of italics, quotations & capitalisation
- Word pairs & homophones
- How to handle numbers & time

…And descriptions of flow, *show not tell,* writing tenses, dialogue handling and more.

Applying these copy-edits to your fiction will allow reviewers and readers to evaluate your novel purely on the strength of your story and not on clumsy and weak prose, overuse of adverbs, repetition and flabbiness.

Your readers may not understand why your fiction is more engaging, but subconsciously they will respond to the improved flow, the more immediate prose and leaner sentences.

All About Copywriting cannot guarantee you marketing success; what it will guarantee is to give your novel the best chance it can get in a tough, competitive and new publishing world.

Getting readers past page one, despite your 'explosive, fast paced hitting-the-ground-running opening', is what this guide is all about.

How are we going to do that?

By using creative writing technique. By demonstrating your writing credentials on not only page one, but all your pages. By showing reviewers and your readers you can write, and write well.

Today it is very easy to self-publish electronically. You can write a story in the morning and publish in the afternoon - and astoundingly, many authors do this. Hundreds of them. The temptation is to publish when the work is far from ready. As a professional independent author, it is your job to avoid this pitfall.

One thing will always stand out above everything else: *Good writing.* Reviewers will always be swayed by good writing. Readers will be drawn into your novels by good writing. I'm going to say it one more time: *Good writing.*

The worst criticism I can imagine for any independent author is that of 'poor technique' - a lack of professionalism. Sure, readers and reviewers may not like the work for any number of reasons, but having a professional approach and applying discipline to your editing process, will maximise your chances of success.

I would go as far to say that no matter how wonderful your plot, story and characters, bad writing will always let you down. *Always.* Conversely, well-edited, considered, professional prose from an independent author who knows their art, can elevate the most poorly imagined story.

This guide won't tell you how to plot, how to create characters, or to write your first kick-ass novel - what it will tell you, however, is how to avoid or fix the numerous pitfalls common to modern novel writing.

But I can do all this online... can't I?

You may think that using any of the many online resources to quickly check your manuscript for unwanted words and phrases such as *that*, *it* and *there are, etc.* is all you have to do to get your novel ship-shape and ready for publication. This guide is superfluous... *isn't it?*

Think again.

These online "resources" rely on "algorithms" - a self-important term for counting words and checking them against a prescribed 'number of appearances per 1000 or so words'.

Do you really think you have somehow fixed/successfully edited your novel because a simple online counting program tells you *all is now okay?* Let's think about that for a moment. A simple counting program...

Let's say you use one of these programs and the results suggest that you are overusing the word *that*. You simply track down every occurrence of *that* in your manuscript, remove enough of them to make the numbers add up and all is well.

Or is it?

I have over twenty years copyediting and writing experience and I strongly believe this approach to be detrimental to fiction writing. For writers to assume that simply deleting a few 'buzz-words' from their manuscript will somehow improve their fiction is laughable.

I'm not knocking these checkers per se, they do have some use - particularly for pointing out repeated words and phrases, but other than that, they should not be relied upon.

For instance, if you are using the word *that* correctly and it is helping sentence flow, there is no need to delete it, regardless of what the numbers say.

We are writers. We are conveying meaning. We are creating emotion, characters and action - it is as far away from a numbers game as you can get.

So how is this guide different?

We will be searching for some of the same buzz-words, but in each and every instance, this guide will explain why we are looking for these words and how they can be misused. It will allow you to make informed decisions about when you need to delete or re-edit and when you can leave your prose alone.

This guide covers areas that no online checker can help you with - italics and capitalisation, how to deal with numbers and time, how to write modern dialogue, how to understand the past and present when using words like *had* and how to use *show not tell* to avoid *passive writing.*

You can do all this in 20,000 words?

This is not a full-on grammar guide and doesn't aim to be. Indeed, there are many hefty reference books out there for you plough through. Instead, this guide focuses on the most common fiction writing pitfalls and gives you targeted advice on how to make your novel a leaner, better, more fulfilling read.

Let's put it in a nutshell:
All About Copywriting is a one-stop copyediting shop to improve your novel before publication.

I want results now!

I cannot give you a definitive time for how long it will take you to implement the fifty-five steps outlined in this guide. The process will take as long as it needs to, but you will see the results immediately. Your novel will read more easily, your writing will have improved flow and your prose will be leaner and more direct.

The next time you write, you will notice how your writing has developed. You will have pinpointed your bad habits and made sure they do not survive past draft one.

Put in the time and your fiction will be the better for it.

Happy copyediting!

INTRODUCTION
Before we start

Let's get this straight from the outset. This guide is not telling you how to write. It will not try to impose any kind of style to your work. It does not in any way set out to constrain you as a writer.

This guide will refer to flow, lazy and bad writing, show not tell, etc. So, before we start copyediting, let's take a look at what is meant by some of these terms.

In this section:

i. Show, not tell
Lights! Camera! Action!... 15

ii. 'Bad writing'
Just what is it?.. 17

iii. Lazy writing
You can do better 19

iv. Narration vs. dialogue & informality
Saying it how it is 21

v. Flow
Following your instincts 25

vi. In summary
Let the copy-editing commence!................................... 26

i. Show, Not Tell

As a writer, you should be aiming to enhance your readership's connection to your fictional world with every piece of descriptive prose, every sentence of dialogue and every paragraph. You must take every opportunity to help them visualise your story.

One of the best ways of accomplishing this is to s*how, not tell*. You have the opportunity to *tell* the reader, second-hand, what is happening or to *show* it them directly.

For the purposes of this guide, we have a love triangle between Bill, his wife Margery and interloper, John.

Telling the reader:
Bill looked at John, who had one of those roguishly attractive faces that got better with age, at his glinting eyes with secrets hidden behind them, at the rough flock of Irish red hair lying across his forehead.

Bill is telling us about John, the grammar is passable and all appears good… but can we do better?

Showing the reader:
John burst into the room, an eternal rogue in his fifties. All red hair and flashing Irish eyes but furtive, with a rake for a smile, and an air of 'I don't give a damn'. He piled into Bill, offering a short stubby hand.

In the above example we can see and almost feel John.

In modern fiction, *showing* is always better than *telling.* You do not always have to *show,* but it is important to know the distinction.

ii. 'Bad Writing'

There are grammar experts out there who can pull apart any great piece of literary work and expose its grammatical flaws. Your work will not be any different - it will contain many flaws.

The trick?
Don't let it bother you too much.

Writing that does not follow the rules or conventions is not, per se, 'bad writing.' Far from it.

Writing should always come from informed choice. Often stylistic concerns and sentence flow will dictate the words you use rather than grammatical rules and convention. But this does not mean that you can abandon grammar altogether. Instead, as a writer, you need to understand these rules and conventions and make informed decisions about when to ignore them.

Once you have familiarised yourself with the fifty-five steps of this guide, you will notice how some of your favourite authors do not always follow these rules and conventions. Their work is still readable and engaging, they are possibly very successful authors…

And so we get to the nitty gritty… Just what is 'bad writing?'

When I refer to 'bad writing' in this guide, I mean: writing that contains unacceptable or poor grammar (grammar that does not work in any context); writing that uses extra and unnecessary words and repeats the same phrases; writing that unintentionally puts the author in a bad light.

By disregarding the basic grammar rules and conventions - or being ignorant of them - writing can become unreadable and jarring.

iii. Lazy Writing

Your Lazy Writing Report Card says: 'Could do better'.

Unlike bad writing, lazy writing is grammatically viable, but there is no wow factor. It is writing that *tells not shows* - writing that is flabby and unimaginative. You may be getting the meaning across to the reader, but you are not fully engaging them.

Let's take an example from *Section Two - "Overused Words"* and in particular, the overuse of <u>was/were</u>:

> John was sitting next to Margery at their table. He was flirting with her and she was laughing at his awful jokes. It was as if Bill was invisible. Everybody in the pub was looking at Bill. They were urging him to do something. To stand up to John.

We get the scene. It's straightforward, but there is no *wow factor* and we are drowning in <u>was</u> and <u>were</u>. Quite frankly, it's lazy.

Let's deal with it:
> John smashed into Margery's dirty sense of humour like a truck into a glass building. She shrieked raucously. Heads turned in the close-mouthed little pub, eyes stabbing at Bill, urging him to act.

By removing all those occurrences of <u>was/were</u>, the paragraph is leaner and draws us into the action.

Do you need to do this with every sentence?
No. This is a style choice. You should always try to show rather than tell, but sometimes, over-elaboration can be detrimental to pace. Sometimes the scene will require simpler sentences. Even so, you should at least consider more engaging ways to say the same thing.

You will always know when a rewrite of a lazy sentence is needed, because you will catch yourself arguing that it's okay to leave it.

Time to step up…

iv. Narrative vs. Dialogue & Informality

The tone and style of your narrative should be consistent throughout your novel. Your characters must talk with their own voice and also be consistent to who they are.

Tell Me A Story…
In a story, the voice of the storyteller, be it First or Third Person - tells us what is going on. They narrate the story.

When writing a novel, you make a decision about the style of narration at the outset. Is it going to be informal or formal? The more informal the narrative is, the more you can break the grammatical conventions and rules. The more traditional/formal the narrative, the more the narrative needs to follow those grammatical conventions and rules.

The problem with narration in bad writing is that it doesn't seem to know where it is coming from. The reasons behind this are:

- Informal, colloquial speech patterns are full of grammatical errors.
- The modern age has spawned email and various social media such as Twitter and Facebook, leading to less formal ways of communicating in writing.

Now, don't get me wrong - I have nothing against daring narrative. Why shouldn't you write your novel in the informal style of an email or a status update? If that is what you want, then do that. Play with the format, play with the rules - create your own aesthetic approach. Your readers will understand that you have made an informed stylistic choice.

It may surprise you to know that Jane Austin, author of *Pride and Prejudice* (1797), was considered an innovative writer in her day. She used techniques and styles from the personal letters of that age (the post box was a revolution). She paused sentences, dealt with conversation in a daring and informal manner and used risqué themes.

Oh... and she invented the modern romance novel in the process.

This is all good, but Jane Austin was making a stylistic choice.

Problems occur in modern fiction when informality leaks unintentionally into your narrative. It weakens your prose and confuses your readers.

Your narrative tone should be set at the outset and should not change throughout your novel (unless there are stylistic reasons for it to do so).

Say What?
When applying the copy-edits of this guide to your novel, you must make a distinction between dialogue and narration/prose.

As stated before, 'Your characters should talk with their own voice and also be consistent to who they are.' <u>People</u>

do not speak in formal ways.

Let's look at an example of colloquial dialogue:
"I just gotta get outta here," said John

Grammatically, this is all over the place (and it's a dreadful cliché - but it illustrates the point). It uses modern spellings, and conjoined words, but let's consider what the fix would look like if we were to deal with this using correct grammar:

"I must leave this place now," said John.

From what we know of John, our roughish Irish man and friend of Bill and Margery, the replacement dialogue does not work for him. It is a bad fit. He wouldn't speak like that.

The replacement dialogue is grammatically correct but it lacks flow. The first sentence wins out.

Keep narrative as narrative and dialogue as dialogue. Do not mix the two. Make sure both are consistent.

v. Flow

We intuitively recognize flowing prose when we read it. But what is it?

Think about sentence structure and length, about paragraphs and pacing, about rhythm and syntax - about sections and your finalised novel - about how your story flows.

Come again?

In its simplest terms, *flow* is writing that does not jar. It has an ease of movement from one word to another, from one sentence and/or event to another. As a writer, you are the one who will make the final decision about your prose - you are in charge of the flow of your novel.

How is flow relevant to copyediting?

The *flow, pace* and *style* of your novel will dictate how it is received by the reader. Sometimes you may feel the need to discard certain grammatical conventions and rules to do this. This is perfectly acceptable. Indeed, by adhering too strictly to the rules of grammar, your writing may suffer.

When applying the fifty-five copy-edits of this guide to your novel, it is important to remember that flow and meaning must come first.

I used the example of the bridging word *that* (Edit #11) in my opening. A word to watch out for, particularly when it is overused, but - and this is very important - it does not mean that you must scour your novel for the offending word and delete all occurrences.

Instead, you should examine every instance of *that* to determine if it is adding or detracting from the *flow* and meaning of any particular sentence.

This is the same for all the individual copy-edits in this guide.

You are aiming for balance - and balance will improve the flow of your novel.

vi. In Summary

You are an artist. Artists don't fit inside boxes. They might throw away the rules to create a masterpiece, but the one thing they all share is an understanding of what the rules are. They all have technique. They have all studied. They all make informed choices. Sometimes they even overuse the word *they* for effect. They can do this.

Let the copyediting commence!

SECTION ONE
Adjectives, adverbs & only

This section looks at the role of adverbs and adjectives in modern fiction, focusing on how they are routinely abused and misused.

In this section:

i. Adjectives
A full, complete, comprehensive, wide-ranging and in depth look at adjectives 29

ii. Common Adjectives
The most commonly abused adjectives 33

iii. Adverbs
And how to be really, totally and utterly sure when to use them 37

iv. Only
A section all on its own 41

i. Adjectives

An adjective is a descriptive word that modifies nouns and pronouns.

Examples:
Glamorous
Arrogant
Grumpy
Bewildered

Margery filled her comfortable house with magnificent Greek busts.

What have I got against adjectives?
Nothing per se, but too many adjectives can make your writing saggy - and may contribute towards a 'no buy'. Modern tastes favour pace instead of the lengthy descriptive passages of old.

Make your adjectives work for you
As a writer, you are trying to get your prose across in the most economical and descriptive way. Overusing adjectives shows a lack of imagination and can make your novel an awkward and dense read.

Become more succinct

Consider the next sentence:
John stood next to the large house wearing a thick coat in the steady rain.

It makes sense, but all those modifying adjectives are unnecessary. A succinct and more descriptive way of handling the adjectives is to be more specific:

> John stood next to the <u>mansion</u> wearing a <u>mackintosh</u> in the <u>drizzle</u>.

One word is better than two. If you're stuck, dig out that Thesaurus.

Repeating, retelling and echoing yourself
Don't nest adjectives with the same meaning. Consider the next sentence:

> Bill had felt <u>anxious</u> and <u>worried</u> for weeks. Over time, his nerves <u>worsened</u>. The sickness <u>intensified</u>.

Yep, Bill is uneasy. And so am I after reading that sentence. *Anxious, worried, nerves* and *sickness* are all telling us the same thing as does *worsened* and *intensified*.

So how do we dig ourselves out of this mire of adjectives? Let's try:

> A storm of anxiety rained down on Bill. Weeks passed, but the clouds did not clear. Would the sun ever shine again?

I replaced the adjective *anxious* with the noun *anxiety*. As we have also lost *worried*, the paragraph now has no adjectives - we are left with a more imaginative and visually compelling statement.

Watch out for redundant adjectives
Some adjective pairs are put in this world just to catch us out. Here are a few examples:

Pitch Black
Large mountain
Burning fire
Various differences
Unexpected accident
Final completion
Close proximity
Blended together
Refer back
Usual habit
Briefly summarise
Exactly the same
True facts

There are many more. Make your own list. Pin it to your work board or monitor. Add to it whenever you find another pair.

EDIT: #1
Search your novel for redundant and repeated adjectives and remove them.
Make note of the adjectives you overuse and watch for them in your future fiction.
Remember: Do not overuse or 'nest' adjectives.

ii. Common Adjectives

Using adjectives with general meanings such as *wonderful, stupid* or *pretty* gives the impression you cannot find the right word. These adjectives are weak because their meaning is broad.

Consider the next sentence:
Margery found her knitting class a <u>wonderful</u> experience.

Knitting can do that... but how lazy is the adjective <u>wonderful</u>? I'm sure Margery can feel a whole range of emotions that are more specific to the exciting new world of her wool class.

It may seem innocuous at first, but you will be surprised at how these adjectives can creep in, breed and take over your fiction. Here is a list of commonly overused adjectives:

Large, small, little, big
Young, old
Hot, cold, warm
Happy, sad
Stupid, thick, wide
Beautiful, wonderful, pretty
Horrid, horrible, terrible, dark

You won't need to replace every instance, but to give you an idea, I was commissioned (a few years ago) to copy-edit a 65,000 word novel from an accomplished writer. I searched the novel for these common adjectives. These were the results for the worst offenders:

> Large: 96
> Small: 58
> Little: 208
> Big: 56
> Old: 57
> Dark: 107
> Hot: 52
> Wide: 49

Of particular interest is *wide*. Forty-nine is the lowest figure, but as it was contained in the phrase 'his/her eyes widened' thirty-six times, I included it as an example of how adjectives can creep into repeated phrases.

By far the most over-used common adjective was *little* with a whopping 208 instances. And, in most instances, the word was deleted without affecting the meaning.

In total there were 683 common adjectives. Let's say for arguments sake, that only half of these needed to be deleted or replaced (unlikely, but let's stick with it). That would leave a whopping 341 opportunities for the author to improve the novel.

Searching for common adjectives (there are a lot of them) and determining their appropriateness can be time-consuming. I've separated the above common adjectives into individual copy-edits. This will help you keep track of the process.

EDIT: #2

Search your novel for the common adjectives: large/small/ little/big.
Replace with more descriptive, less common adjectives, find a more specific noun, or delete.

EDIT: #3

Search your novel for the common adjectives: young/old.
Replace with more descriptive, less common adjectives, find a more specific noun, or delete.

EDIT: #4

Search your novel for the common adjectives: hot/cold/ warm.
Replace with more descriptive, less common adjectives, find a more specific noun, or delete.

EDIT: #5

Search your novel for the common adjectives: happy/sad.
Replace with more descriptive, less common adjectives, find a more specific noun, or delete.

EDIT: #6

Search your novel for the common adjectives: stupid/thick/ wide.
Replace with more descriptive, less common adjectives, find a more specific noun, or delete.

EDIT: #7

Search your novel for the common adjectives: <u>beautiful/ wonderful/pretty</u>.
Replace with more descriptive, less common adjectives, find a more specific noun, or delete.

EDIT: #8

Search your novel for the common adjectives: <u>horrid/ horrible/terrible/dark</u>.
Replace with more descriptive, less common adjectives, find a more specific noun, or delete.

iii. Adverbs

An adverb modifies a verb or adjective to tell you *how* someone did something.

Examples:
Smoothly
Quietly
Angrily

Bill laughed <u>loudly</u>. Margery waved a <u>beautifully</u> manicured hand <u>irritatingly</u> and <u>abruptly</u> left the room.

Adverbs… good or bad?
Using '<u>ly</u>' ending adverbs is not against the rules of English language. Indeed, you can find a list of famous authors who use these adverbs - albeit sparingly. If you go back twenty or so years, adverbs were used more often, particularly in schlocky science fiction and fantasy of that period. But times have changed. Overuse of adverbs is viewed negatively.

But you like using adverbs
Sometimes a well-placed and specific adverb or adjective strengthens or clarifies an image. For the majority of the time, they do not. Many writers mistakenly believe that using adverbs makes their writing more descriptive.

A little heads up: *It doesn't.*

A lot of bad writers (and I'm using the term 'bad writers' for those who defend adverbs because, 'I can't say what

I want to say without using them') are not aware that professional editors rarely tolerate them. If you are paying for editing services, you will be wasting their valuable time and your money.

This guide is not telling you what to write. Use adverbs as much as you want, but understand that they may have a negative impact on the way your fiction is perceived.

The problem with ly ending adverbs?

Most adverbs are totally unnecessary. As is the adverb *totally* in the opening sentence of this paragraph. How much more *unnecessary* can you get? You can't. The adverb *totally* is redundant.

> **Try these examples:**
> Effortlessly easy
> The horn blared loudly
> Creeping stealthily
> Running quickly

Adverbs also crop up as speech modifiers. Consider:

"Come here," John whispered quietly.

Yes, John, we know you've lowered your voice - how else are you going to whisper?

The above are examples of adverbs modifying verbs where the adverb is redundant, but let's not stop there. Let's look at how unnecessary they are in general writing.

Margery caught the keys <u>expertly</u>
John smiled <u>thinly</u>
Bill answered <u>smoothly</u>
"I love you," Margery said <u>tenderly</u>

Can we remove the above adverbs without losing the meaning? Yes we can. If the meaning is not changed, remove the adverb.

If you are unsure about removing adverbs, I suggest completing the next edit and saving the result as a copy. Revisit it after a few days and give it a re-read. You should notice that your prose is easier to read and that your meaning has not suffered.

EDIT: #9

Search your novel for words ending in <u>ly</u>.
Is the adverb needed? Can you remove it and keep the meaning? Delete where necessary.
Remember: Use adverbs sparingly.

iv. Only

The word *only* is often used in fiction in an unclear manner. It describes or modifies the word or phrase/clause right after it. Also means: alone, solely, no other.

Let's see how it works:

1. Only Margery slapped Bill in the face.
Meaning: Margery slapped Bill in the face and no one else did.

2. Margery slapped only Bill in the face.
Meaning: Margery Slapped Bill in the face and no one else. Everyone else is safe from Margery's face slapping antics.

3. Margery slapped Bill only in the face.
Meaning: Margery Slapped Bill in the face and nowhere else on his body.

4. Margery only slapped Bill in the face.
Meaning: Have you spotted it? This can have two meanings:

a. It could mean Margery slapped Bill in his face and didn't do anything else like kick him in the shins.

b. On the other hand, it could mean Margery slapped Bill in the face and did nothing else to his face - like punch or kick it.

As you can see, Margery is quite a violent girl, but she does highlight how using <u>only</u> can be a tricky affair. Make sure you are using this modifier correctly.

EDIT: #10

Search your novel for <u>only.</u>

Put the adverb <u>only</u> as close as possible to what it is modifying. If in doubt delete/re-write.

SECTION TWO
Overused Words

A list of commonly overused words and phrases that can clog up, slow down and ruin your prose - and when and how to deal with them.

In this section:

i. That
Is that what we want? 45

ii. Was/Were
That was the was that was 51

iii. There is/There are/It is
There is no excuse for using these phrases 55

iv. It
Just what is it? 59

v. Had
A journey into time 63

vi. Up, Down, Inside & Out
This may be beneath you 69

vii. Of
Of all the bars 73

i. That

The word that can sometimes be overused in fiction writing. It is a bridging word that has gone - in many an editor's opinion - a bridge too far. But when should we use or omit it? The answer is a tricky one. Most of the time, it will be up to you.

The two most important things we need to know about that are:

1. Is that needed to make sense of the sentence?
2. Does removing that affect sentence flow?

Do we need that?
Let's start off with a simple sentence:

> Bill said that it was time Margery put her marriage first.

The above example is grammatically correct, but is that necessary to make sense of the sentence? Can we omit that without losing the meaning? Let's take a look:

> Bill said it was time Margery put her marriage first.

As we can see, the examples work as well as each other. Both are grammatically acceptable. However, when streamlining a novel, you should always aim to remove as many redundant words as possible. In this instance, I would suggest deleting the unnecessary that as it is adding nothing to the sentence.

When to keep <u>that</u> to aid sentence flow

When writers find out about <u>that</u>, they often scour their manuscripts for the offending word and over-delete leading to odd sounding sentences.

<u>That</u> has a part to play in many sentences. Some sentences will sound odd with <u>that</u> missing, particularly in association with non-bridge verbs like *understood*.

Example:
John understood Bill wanted go fishing with him.

We get it, but the flow is wrong. The missing <u>that</u> after the verb *understood* jars. It needs a <u>that</u> to give the sentence flow:

John understood <u>that</u> Bill wanted go fishing with him.

Yes, that's better.

Let's try another example with a noun:
The fact John showed no respect annoyed Bill.

This, again, sounds off-kilter. It needs a <u>that</u> after the noun:

The fact <u>that</u> John showed no respect annoyed Bill.

Again, the flow is improved.

One more example with an adjective:
Bill was annoyed John spelled his name incorrectly.

Let's add a that:
Bill was annoyed that John spelled his name incorrectly.

The above examples all feature instances where that is needed to give the sentence flow, but using that with other non-bridging verbs, nouns and adjectives may give the opposite result. You may decide a sentence does not need that.

The choice is yours.

Paired thats
Sometimes the sentence only needs one that. In the below example, there is an accidental extra that. Can you spot which one it is?

Bill shouted that John's house sign had a deliberate mistake and that if he didn't change it, there would be trouble.

The first that is necessary, the second is redundant.

Let's replace the second that with a comma:
Bill shouted that John's house sign had a deliberate mistake and, if he didn't change it, there would be trouble.

Who is that?
It is common in modern speech to refer to people as that when the correct term is who. In prose, you need to know when to use that and when to use who.

Example of misuse:
John is the guy that admires Margery.

Yeah. At first glance this looks correct, but it is bad writing. The sentence should say:

John is the guy who admires Margery.

This is a very simple error that is easy to correct.

That vs. Which
The simple rule is:

Use that when it is referring to the subject of the sentence.

Use which when it is referring to the object of the sentence.

Example of that usage:
This is the book that tells me how to copy-edit.

In the above sentence, that refers to the subject (the book) which is actively doing something.

Example of which usage:
This is the book which was given to me by a friend.

In the above sentence, the book is now the object. The friend is the one who doing the action (giving).

...And that, as they say, is that.

EDIT: #11

Search your novel for <u>that</u>.

Examine every occurrence of <u>that</u>.

Does removing <u>that</u> affect the flow of the sentence? If not, then delete.

Does <u>that</u> refer to a person? If so, change to <u>who</u>.

Should you be using <u>which</u>?

Remember: Do not remove <u>that</u> for the sake of it. The sentence must make sense and read well.

ii. Was/Were

We are all guilty of overusing <u>was</u> and <u>were</u>. But we don't need to hang our heads in shame. They are usually the symptom of a first draft - and are easily fixed. If they are still present in numbers in your finished writing - they need to be dealt with.

> **Example:**
> John <u>was</u> sitting next to Margery. He <u>was</u> flirting with her and she <u>was</u> laughing at his awful jokes. It <u>was</u> as if Bill was invisible. Everybody in the pub <u>was</u> looking at Bill. They <u>were</u> telling him to do something. To stand up to John.

The above is an example of Lazy Writing - we are drowning in <u>was</u> and <u>were</u>.

Nasty.

What is the problem with <u>was</u>/<u>were</u>?
The problem is Passive Writing. This is a big can-of-worms for fiction writers. The best way to describe it is:

> **Passive Writing** pushes the reader away from the action.

> **Active Writing** puts the reader in amongst the action.

Passive Writing is *telling* not *showing*. Whenever possible, you must try to *show*.

Consider the first sentence of the example paragraph:
John <u>was sitting</u> next to Margery.

We can replace this with an active version saying the same thing:

John <u>sat</u> next to Margery.

Let's look at the second sentence:
He <u>was flirting</u> with her and she <u>was laughing</u> at his awful jokes.

We can change this in the same way, but it is clunky:

He flirted with her and she laughed at his awful jokes.

In situations like this, it's probably best to try reworking the paragraph as a whole with the emphasis on *show not tell:*

John smashed into Margery's dirty sense of humour like a truck into a glass building. She shrieked raucously. Heads turned in the close-mouthed little pub, eyes stabbing at Bill, urging him to act.

Okay, the revised sentences need a little work, but by removing all those occurrences of <u>was/were</u>, the paragraph is leaner and draws us in to the action.

That was the <u>was</u> that <u>was</u>
You cannot eliminate every <u>was/were</u> from your manuscript

and don't try to. It is also acceptable to have passive sentences in your fiction as long as they do not dominate.

EDIT: #12

Search your novel for was/were.

If you can replace was/were with more *active* prose that *shows* rather than *tells,* do so.

Remember: Do not change if the flow feels right. However, removing passive sentences and was/were will give your fiction a leaner feel and draw your readers into the action.

iii. There is/There are/It is

Using <u>there is/there are/it is</u> is correct English, but overuse is poor writing and shows bad style.

> **Example:**
> "<u>It is</u> a truth universally acknowledged, that a single man in possession of a good fortune must be in want of a wife."

Hang on! Yes, of course, this is the first line from *Pride and Prejudice* by Jane Austin, but it does not mean that you can put this phrase into your manuscripts willy-nilly.

But if it's good enough for Jane Austin...
This argument can be applied to any of the copyediting suggestions in this guide. Yes, they are all *suggestions*. You do not have to follow any of them. But understand that the overuse of <u>there is/there are/it is</u> is seen by many as Bad Writing.

We are trying to give your work the best chance it can get. Eliminating and rewriting these instances will do no harm to your novel.

Okay...Why?

Quite simply, the combination of *Subject* <u>there/it</u> and *Verb* <u>are/is</u> tells the reader nothing. They do not convey any important information. <u>*They are*</u> a waste of space.

Overuse signifies a writer too languid to find a more

informative subject and verb combination.

Example:
There are too many gnomes in Bill's garden.

The Fix:
Bill's garden contains too many gnomes.

Example:
There are three people in this relationship who are important.

The Fix:
The three characters in this relationship are important.

Example:
It is Margery who I love.

The Fix:
I love Margery.

As you can see, the fixes are relatively simple, but unimaginative.

See every instance of there is/there are/it is as an opportunity to rewrite and improve your novel.

When is it okay to use it is?
Just to confuse the matter, it is perfectly okay to use it is when talking about days, dates, distances, the weather and time.

Examples:

<u>It is</u> Thursday all day.

<u>It is</u> September.

<u>It is</u> five miles to John's canal boat.

<u>It is</u> raining in Bill's garden.

<u>It is</u> three o'clock in the afternoon.

However, this is Lazy Writing. The examples can be written more imaginatively.

EDIT: #13

Search your novel/fiction for <u>there is, there are</u> and <u>it is</u>. Rewrite most, if not all instances. If used in speech, look at *flow* and *character*.

Remember: <u>There is/are</u> and <u>it is</u> mostly say nothing and relying on them to get across your meaning will not score you many points with your reviewers and readership.

iv. It

The main problem with <u>it</u> comes from the fact that it is a pronoun like he/she/you and not a noun like *tree* or *fish* or *Saturn*. It tells us nothing unless it is associated with the subject.

Consider this sentence:
Bill built a statue of the Goddess Aphrodite in his garden, hoping to attract the lovely Margery. <u>It</u> measured ten feet in height and weighed over fifty pounds.

What is wrong with this statement? Absolutely nothing. The sentence is grammatically correct. The use of <u>it</u> points to the *subject* - Bill's statue, which is all well and good. Now let us continue:

Bill built a statue of the Goddess Aphrodite in his garden, hoping to attract the lovely Margery. <u>It</u> measured ten feet in height and weighed over fifty pounds. Everyone was amazed by <u>it</u>. All except John who thought <u>it</u> crass and ugly.

Now we are starting to see the cracks appear. The writer is relying on the non-descriptive <u>it</u> too heavily. Instead of exploiting the opportunity to describe this incredible statue further, the writer has copped out.

Let's try it again:
Bill built a statue of the Goddess Aphrodite in his garden, hoping to attract the lovely Margery. <u>The</u>

<u>sculpture</u> measured ten feet in height and weighed over fifty pounds. Everyone was amazed by the <u>intricate chiselling and fine craftsmanship of Aphrodite's considerable curves</u>. All except John who thought <u>the effigy</u> crass and ugly.

Yes, we certainly get a better idea about Bill's sculpture from the enhanced description. Notice also the replacement of <u>it</u> by *sculpture* and *effigy*.

Is it, Its, It's Or Its'?
Using <u>its</u> and <u>it's</u> incorrectly is a very common error in English writing.

<u>Its'</u> - There is no such word as <u>its'</u>.
<u>Its</u> - is the possessive form of <u>it</u> (like his or her).
<u>It's</u> - a contraction of <u>it is</u>. When you see the apostrophe, you should think *it is*.

Examples:
Bill's garden had <u>its</u> own set of homemade gnomes.
"Making gnomes is not a silly hobby," said Bill, "<u>it's</u> an art."

<u>Is it</u> starting to make sense?

EDIT: #14
Search your novel for <u>it</u>.
Replace with more descriptive prose or find another way of saying the sentence.
Check for correct usage of <u>its</u> and <u>it's</u>.
Remember: <u>It</u> on its own says nothing.

v. Had

Before we delve into the use of <u>had</u> - let's take a quick look at how tense is handled in fiction.

The Present Tense
The narrator tells us the story as it happens.

Simple Past
The narrator tells us a story that has already happened.

The Pluperfect Tense (Deep Past)
This relates to action completed further back in time than Simple Past and refers to past participle verbs and the auxiliary word <u>had</u>.

Let's delve a little deeper.

Present Tense
Events happening in the *now.*

Example:
Bill <u>enters</u> John's garden and <u>burns</u> down his shed.

Present Tense adds an immediacy that can be very powerful.

Simple Past
Retelling events that have already happened.

Example:
Bill <u>entered</u> John's garden and <u>burned</u> down his shed.

The Pluperfect Tense (Deep Past)

Don't be put off by the strangeness of this word. It refers to your <u>had</u> verbs - where Deep Past action takes place *before* Simple Past.

> **Example:**
> Bill <u>had entered</u> John's garden and <u>had burned</u> down his shed.

Had enough?

<u>Had</u> is (often) a word pertaining to Deep Past. There is nothing wrong with this word as long as it is used effectively. Problems arise when Deep Past is overused - writers fall into the trap of *telling* and not *showing*.

It all happened a long time ago.

Characters have a history - things happened to them.

When writing fiction, the most immediate way of grabbing your audience is to place your action in Simple Past.

So how do we deal with *less recent events?*

> **Example:**
> The problems with Margery <u>had</u> started yesterday. Bill <u>had</u> woken to find his wife missing. She <u>had</u> left him a note on his pillow, saying she <u>had</u> needed a break. John <u>had</u> offered her his little narrow boat he <u>had</u> moored on the river.

This is a common overuse of <u>had</u> and Deep Past. The problem is that our author is writing exclusively in Deep

Past and feels the need to emphasise this tense by the repeated use of <u>had</u>.

You do not need to do this.

Let's try using only one <u>had</u>. This will put us in Deep Past. Once there, I will move the narrative back to Simple Past without losing the sense we are still in Deep Past.

> The problems with Margery <u>had</u> started yesterday. Bill woke to find his wife missing, a note on his pillow:

> 'I need a break. John is offering me his narrow boat for a week. I'm going to take up his offer. A week by the river on my own will do us both good. Love, M x'

It's not going so well for Bill is it? And I've got my suspicions about John's motivation… But that aside, being in the Simple Past *of yesterday* reads better.

I would even go as far as to remove the first <u>had</u> - as it is not needed:

> The problems with Margery started yesterday. Bill woke to find his wife missing, a note on his pillow:

> 'I need a break. John is offering me his narrow boat for a week. I'm going to take up his offer. A week by the river on my own will do us both good. Love, M x'

A step too far? That's for you to decide. Just be aware that an over-reliance of Deep Past at the expense of action can cost you readers and sales.

Where did the Past go?
Relying on Deep Past is a common error for some writers. Indeed, they jump straight to Deep Past when they should be using Simple Past.

> **Example:**
> John owned a narrow boat he <u>had</u> purchased years ago.
>
> We can see it straight away. That <u>had</u> is not needed. Let's get rid.
>
> John owned a narrow boat purchased years ago.

We dumped the <u>had</u> and no longer needed the redundant <u>he</u> as John is identified as the subject of the sentence. All is well.

Flashbacks
There is no need to write all your flashbacks in Deep Past. In fact, it is desirable to not do so.

A simple technique is to introduce the flashback with a line or two of introductory text and then either leave a double space, three asterisks or an ellipsis.

The reader will understand this convention. You can then write the flashback in Simple Past.

Double space:
Margery remembered the events on the canal boat and frowned.

John was full of smiles as he picked her up in his open top sports car. But his mood changed as soon as he took the helm of his boat. Captain John was bossy. Margery found herself at his beck and call and did not like it.

Asterisks:
Margery remembered the events on the canal boat and frowned.

***

John was full of smiles as he picked her up in his open top sports car. But his mood changed as soon as he took the helm of his boat. Captain John was bossy. Margery found herself at his beck and call and did not like it.

Ellipsis:
Margery remembered the events on the canal boat and frowned...

John was full of smiles as he picked her up in his open top sports car. But his mood changed as soon as took the helm of his boat. Captain John was bossy. Margery found herself at his beck and call and did not like it.

<u>Had</u> enough?

EDIT: #15

Search your novel for <u>had</u>.

Move past paragraphs and sections into Simple Past by managing your <u>hads</u> effectively.

Delete unnecessary <u>hads</u> from Simple Past & Deep Past.

Remember: You should always be actively trying to *show not tell*, Over-reliance on <u>hads</u> will cost you readers and sales.

vi. Up, Down, Inside & Out

Words that indicate a location can be overused and/or be unnecessary in your fiction. If you are not careful, you can end up scattering these prepositions throughout your writing when they serve no discernible purpose.

It is important to search your manuscript for needless common prepositions.

Example:
Bill focused <u>in on</u> John's motives.

The <u>in</u> is not needed and can be deleted:

Bill focused <u>on</u> John's motives.

Other examples:
John travelled <u>out</u> to his boat.
Bill went <u>in</u> through the door

In the above examples we can lose the needless propositions without affecting the sentence meaning:

John travelled to his boat.
Bill went through the door

End of sentence prepositions

The above words are all examples of prepositions. At one time, people were taught to never end a sentence with a preposition, but this view is archaic. However, it still crops up as an issue for fiction writers who are unsure if this is 'good writing'. Be assured, end of sentence propositions are perfectly acceptable.

Examples:
Bill hoped Margery would cheer up.
Bill went to John's house to tell him to leave off.
"What do you need to go to John's for?"

Sometimes, trying to rewrite a sentence to avoid an end of sentence preposition can lead to odd sounding prose.

Example:
Bill hoped Margery up would cheer.

We would never speak or write a sentence like the above example, however, always be alert for end of sentence prepositions. They do not indicate bad writing, but sometimes the sentence will benefit from a revision.

Common prepositions to watch out for:
Up/Down
In/Out
On/off
Over/Under/Below/Beneath

Searching for these individual propositions and determining their appropriateness can be time-consuming. I've separated the above into individual copy-edits. This will help you keep track of the process.

EDIT: #16

Search your novel for <u>up</u> and <u>down</u> including <u>upwards</u> and <u>downwards</u>.
Is the preposition needed? If not remove or rewrite.

EDIT: #17

Search your novel for <u>in</u> and <u>out</u> including <u>inwards</u>, <u>outwards</u>, <u>inside</u> and <u>outside</u>.
Is the preposition needed? If not remove or rewrite.

EDIT: #18

Search your novel for <u>over/under/below/beneath</u>.
Is the preposition needed? If not remove or rewrite.

EDIT: #19

Search your novel for <u>on</u> and <u>off</u> including <u>onwards</u>.
Is the preposition needed? If not remove or rewrite.

vii. Of

<u>Of</u> is another preposition we should try to avoid.

Why?

Because it can add unnecessary elaboration leading to passive writing.

Example:
John is the nemesis <u>of</u> Bill.

John would be Bill's nemesis if he wrote like that. Let's make the obvious fix:

John is Bill's nemesis.

Another Example:
Bill built a statue <u>of</u> the Goddess Aphrodite in his garden, hoping to attract the lovely Margery.

In the above sentence, <u>of</u> is used correctly. Bill has built an actual statue <u>of</u> Aphrodite. It can't be rewritten effectively and does not need an edit.

Get Off my Of
It is common for <u>of</u> to become accidentally replaced with *off* and visa-versa. These can be tricky to spot as your spell-checker will not flag them up.

However, modern grammar indicators in word processing programs (which you should never rely on) underline propositions they *think* are being used improperly. You can search for them by tweaking your grammar preferences in your word processor.

EDIT: #20
Search your novel for <u>of</u>.
Remove when unnecessary.
Is the sentence *active* or *passive?* If *passive* then rewrite.
Remember: Make sure you have not confused <u>of</u> with *off.*

SECTION THREE
"What is more boring than watching paint dry?"

The answer? *Watching someone else watch paint dry.* This section deals with words and phrases whose only function is to remove the reader from the action.

Yes, it's more of that *show not tell* malarkey. Dampening the impact of your action by filtering it through someone else's perceptions, is less than compelling.

In this section:

i. Felt/Feel/Feeling
A lack of emotion? 77

ii. Look/Looked/Looking
Look away now 81

iii. Watch/Notice/Observe
Blink and you won't miss it 85

iv. See/Saw
The ups and downs 87

v. Hear/Heard
We're not listening 89

vi. Smell/Taste
Something iffy in the air 91

vii. Knew/Know
You do know that I know that you know? 93

If you are writing in First Person, or Third Person Limited (where everything is experienced through your main character), filtering the world through your main character's senses is unavoidable. Try more inventive ways of describing the action.

A good way to apply this section to your writing, is to ask yourself the question: *is my character using any of his or her senses to tell us things?* If they are - please make them stop!

i. Felt/Feel/Feeling

These verbs are weak and push your prose towards passivity. Don't *tell* the reader what someone is feeling. Instead, *show* us the emotion. Over-using Felt/Feel/Feeling will not score you many points with editors or impress your readers.

Can't shake the feeling?
Yes you can. And here's how.

> **Example:**
> John put his arm around Margery. Bill felt a wave of jealousy wash over him.

The main word here is *jealousy*. Bill is jealous. Using felt moves the reader one step away from the emotion.

> **Let's fix the sentence:**
> John put his arm around Margery. A wave of jealousy washed over Bill.

Both sentences say the same thing, yet the revised version is more immediate.

> **Let's try another:**
> John had a feeling Bill was watching him.

This is a double-whammy. The had puts us in the Deep Past (pluperfect), removing us from the action, whilst John's feeling - experiencing the action from his perspective - places the reader yet another step away. Golly.

Let's try the same prose using Simple Past:
John <u>felt</u> Bill watching him.

This is grammatically correct, but we are using <u>felt</u> which removes us from the action.

Let's fix this with *show not tell*:
Bill's stabbing eyes prickled the back of John's neck.

The fix puts us into the *action* and creates a more compelling description.

Feeling good?
Are there any instances where use of <u>felt/feel/feeling</u> is not bad writing? Yes. If your character *physically feels* something or someone:

Example:
Bill <u>felt</u> for loose change in his trouser pocket.

In this instance, the use of <u>felt</u> is fine, but not over-imaginative. We could also say:

Bill <u>grasped</u> for loose change in his trouser pocket.

<u>Felt/feel/feeling</u> are feeble words to use, particularly when the English Language provides us with a multitude of synonyms.

Try:
Caressed, handled, fondled, fingered, etc.

EDIT: #21

Search your novel for <u>felt/feel/feeling</u>.

Replace all with more descriptive prose or find another way of saying the sentence.

Remember: Using <u>felt/feel/feeling</u> adds nothing to your writing.

ii. Look/Looked/Looking

Why *tell* us someone is looking at something when you can *show* us what they are looking at?

Example:
Bill <u>looked</u> at the winding ravine, descending hundreds of feet in a single steep drop.

Thanks Bill, but why won't you let us see it for ourselves?

Bill balanced on the lip of a winding ravine descending hundreds of feet in a single steep drop.

By balancing Bill on the lip of the ravine we have added an extra *action* element to the description: Bill might fall or... *will he jump?*

Let's try another:
Bill had a <u>look</u> of sadness on his face.

I would too, if I had submitted this to an editor. Once again the writer is falling into the trap of *telling not showing.* Let's fix this monstrosity quickly:

A murky river washed over Bill, drowning him in eddies of despair.

The sentence could also do with a little work – 'murky river'? Maybe I could use better adjectives? But at least I am attempting to *show not tell.* The reader is not imagining Bill's sad face, but experiencing his emotion directly.

The eyes have it

There is no doubt about it, your characters have eyes, which means they can do a hell of a lot of <u>looking</u>. The main problem? …*That's all they do in bad fiction.*

> **Example:**
> Margery <u>looked</u> at John. He <u>looked</u> back at her, his eyes returning her hungry <u>look</u>.

It is rare to find so many <u>looks</u> in a paragraph. But using <u>look</u> is a lazy option when you can use *action* to convey the moment.

> **Let's fix the paragraph:**
> Margery focused on John. His intent eyes mirrored her hunger.

I don't know about you, but I'm certainly getting more of a tingle from the revised version. The first attempt would slow your heartbeat, the second speed it up.

Take a look, peek and glance at synonyms

There are hundreds of words more specific than <u>look/looked/looking</u>. Please, use a Thesaurus.

> **Example:**
> Margery <u>looked</u> at Bill angrily.

This writer clearly is not interested in creating pictures with words. <u>Looked</u> and *angrily* must be to the two most generic descriptions you can use to express emotion in poor fiction.

The sentence can be rewritten as:
Margery *glowered* at Bill.

The meaning is the same, but at least the writer has used an actual facial expression. The revision works, but also consider a further edit:

> Bill's cruel words sliced through Margery like hot shards, twisting her expression into one of pure fury.

Watch out Bill!

Examples of synonyms:

> **To look at:** gaze, stare, gape, glare, glower, scowl, frown, grimace, gawk, ogle, etc.
>
> **A type of look:** appearance, expression, air, aspect, mien, bearing, demeanour, posture, etc.

Why are you so angry looking?
Because you are using <u>looking</u> when you don't need to. That's why.

An extra little note - some writers, myself included - can fall into the habit of adding an extra <u>looking</u> in their descriptive sentences.

> **Some examples.**
> Margery was a plain <u>looking</u> girl.
> John, an assured <u>looking</u> middle-aged man.
> Bill, unhappy <u>looking</u> and anxious, followed Margery.

In the above cases <u>looking</u> is superfluous.

> **Let's remove the extra baggage:**
> Margery was a plain girl.
> John, an assured middle-aged man.
> Bill, unhappy and anxious, followed Margery.

EDIT: #22

Search your novel for <u>look/looked/looking</u>.
Revise most instances into *action*.
When necessary, replace with more descriptive synonyms.

iii. Watch/Notice/Observe

I debated lumping watch/notice/observe with <u>look/looked/looking</u> as in many respects they are the same - viewing from a distance *telling* the reader rather than *showing* and pushing us away from the *action*.

However, as this is a practical guide to fix your novel, I decided this works best as a separate step.

<u>Watch/notice/observe</u> are weak verbs - giving rise to weak prose and weak writing. The last thing we need is to encounter characters who are watching.

Example:
Bill <u>watched</u> John and Margery exit the canal boat arm in arm and his heart sank.

How about:

John and Margery exited the canal boat arm in arm. Bill's heart sank.

Not a great sentence, but a lot better than it was before.

Example:
Bill <u>noticed</u> Margery blush under his accusing glare.

How about:

Margery blushed under Bill's accusing glare.

Again, the fix is simple and it brings the reader closer to the action.

Example:
John <u>observed</u> Bill breaking into his locked shed.

We need to know that John has spotted Bill and his shed-breaking antics, but...

Bill broke into John's locked shed.

...does not convey the right information. How do we say, *John observed Bill*, without actually saying, *John observed Bill?*

How about:
The flash of a torch in the garden alerted John to his jealous neighbour's presence. A crack of wood and Bill gained access to his locked shed.

By focusing on the action, we have a better sense of the scene.

EDIT: #23
Search your novel for <u>watch/notice/observe</u>.
Revise most instances into *action*.
When necessary, replace with more descriptive synonyms.

iv. See/Saw

If a character is in a scene with people or things, we do not need to be told they are <u>seeing</u> them.

I saw it on the telly
One of the commonest mistakes new screenwriters make is telling us what characters can <u>see</u>.

Screenplay Example:

Margery: Look at the shed, John! Bill has smashed the door in and set fire to it.

John: And all my gardening magazines are strewn all over the lawn.

So you're wondering - why all this scriptwriting nonsense? I'm using it to illustrate a simple point. All the dialogue in the above screenplay is superfluous. The viewer can <u>see</u> the smashed shed door, the smoking roof and the magazines - we do not need to be *told* it.

The same can be said for the use of <u>see/saw</u>. We do not need to be told someone is <u>seeing</u> something, when we know they can see it.

Example:
John <u>saw</u> Margery smile.

I'm sure he did. He is there, looking at Margery. Do we need to <u>see</u> through John's eyes? Nope.

How about:
Margery smiled.

The introductory <u>John saw</u> is redundant. We have fixed the sentence, but it's still using the generic word *smile*. Quite frankly, it's boring. Let's ditch the simple fix and go for a rewrite:

> Margery hunched her shoulders, trying to suppress a giggle.

…And we're back to *show not tell*.

EDIT: #24

Search your novel for <u>see/saw</u>.
Revise most instances into *action*.
When necessary, replace with more descriptive synonyms.

v. Hear/Heard

As we are treading the same territory as see/saw, I won't go into great detail. The reader understands that a character (unless told differently) can hear things, so we don't need to be told he can hear them.

Example:
Bill heard blaring police sirens echoing in the distance. Coming closer. Stopping outside his house.

Again, we do not need to know Bill heard anything. Let's deal with this quickly:

A blaring police siren echoed in the distance. Coming closer. Stopping outside Bill's house.

Example:
"I can hear sirens," said Margery. "Tell me you didn't call the police, John?"

Let's remove the unwanted hear:

"Sirens?" said Margery. "Tell me you didn't call the police, John?"

EDIT: #25
Search your novel for hear/heard.
Revise most instances into *action*.
When necessary, replace with more descriptive synonyms.

vi. Smell/Taste

Like hearing and seeing, <u>smell/taste</u> is another of the human senses employed by bad writers to keep us away from the action.

> **Example:**
> John could <u>smell</u> the rank odour of petrol. This was no accidental fire.

We do not need to a second-hand description. Describing the smell directly gives us more to play with:

> The rank odour of petrol hung over the smouldering remains like an accusing finger.

John is not in the equation, the description is enough.

> **Example:**
> Bill ate the Meal-For-One mechanically. It had no <u>taste</u>.

The above example is using *action,* but we are still confronted with the generic phrase *no <u>taste</u>*.

Let's take a look at our Thesaurus:

> Bill ate the watery Meal-For-One mechanically.

Here, I've used a synonym for tasteless, other synonyms are bland, insipid, flat - all superior to *no <u>taste</u>*.

EDIT: #26

Search your novel for <u>smell/taste</u>.

Revise most instances into action.

When necessary, replace with more descriptive synonyms.

vii. Knew/Know

Knew/know gives us passive, second-hand information. If the character knows something it is likely, the reader will know it as well.

Other words to watch out for: *claimed* and *believed*.

Example:
Bill knew Margery had the hots for John.

Did he? If you've been following our little love triangle, you will know the above statement is superfluous. Why tell us the reader something we have already discovered? It's pointless. This sentence can be deleted as it is saying nothing.

Another Example:
"I know you have been seeing John," said Bill.

Do we need *I know* to make the above sentence work? Let's remove it and see how much more powerful Bill's accusation can be:

"You have been seeing John," said Bill.

The dialogue is more immediate and has more punch.

As we are dealing with speech, you might consider the use of *I know* to be more colloquial, to follow natural speaking patterns. The choice is yours. Searching all of your manuscript will give you an indication of how to balance these out.

The use of <u>knew/know</u> is sometimes necessary, but its presence alone should invoke an examination.

EDIT: #27

Search your novel for <u>knew/know</u> and also claim/claimed, believe/believed.

Revise most instances into *action*.

When necessary, replace with more descriptive synonyms.

SECTION FOUR
"Italics, Quotation Marks & Capitalisation"

There is no excuse for not knowing when to use italics, quotation marks and capitalisation in modern fiction, but you would be surprised by how many writers do not do their homework on this subject. There are countless resources on this subject, so instead of going through lists of examples, I will stick to the main areas.

In this section:

i. Emphasis
You 'KNOW' what I mean? 97

ii. Planes, Trains & Automobiles
What's in a name? 103

iii. Foreign Words, Sounds & Letters
Harrumph 107

iv. Family Names & Titles
Keeping mum 109

v. Directions
Advice on how not to get lost 111

vi. Numbers, Dates & Times
It will all add up 113

I'm far from perfect with my italics and quotation marks and get mixed up easily, but when I'm copyediting, I always make sure I check them. I'd be a fool not to.

NB. Even though I am British, I am using the American convention of double quotation marks for speech and single quotation marks for definitions:

"My favourite quote is, 'Live life to the fullest', by Ernest Hemingway," said Kev.

You may use the British way, which is: 'My favourite quote is, "Live life to the fullest", by Ernest Hemingway,' said Kev.

Understand that whatever your style of punctuation (" " vs. ' ') the same rules apply.

Make sure you are consistent in their use.

i. Emphasis

A true story: At school, when I was ten years old, my teacher told me to write out all the words in italics from my English exercise book. And I did write them out - *in italics*. Took me ages. Especially all those fiddly *f*s. I was a literal-minded child...

Putting a slant on things

One of the most common uses of italics is to place emphasis on *certain* words in your prose. As I just did with the word *certain*. We do this to draw the reader's attention to a particular word in our sentence. This can be because the word is important or because you are referencing a word directly.

Examples:
Why did John use the word *married?*

The above sentence references the word *married* directly.

There is something *underhand* about John.

The above example is emphasising how Bill perceives John.

You can use single quotation marks to also highlight 'certain' words. This is an acceptable way of adding emphasis, but 'overuse' can be 'jarring' to the 'reader' and should be 'avoided':

Bill knew the words for John: 'underhand', 'sleazy'

and 'wicked'. They all added up to one thing: 'wife stealer'.

As you can see - all those quotation marks are getting in the way.

Let's consider the same sentence using italics for emphasis:

> Bill knew the words for John: *underhand, sleazy* and *wicked*. They all added up to one thing: *wife stealer*.

Yes, that's better. But do we need to emphasise them all? Let's try moving the emphasis to the end of the sentence:

> Bill knew the words for John: underhand, sleazy and wicked. They all added up to one thing: *wife stealer*.

In the last example, I've made a stylistic choice on where to place the emphasis, although it is grammatically correct to emphasise them all.

Over-emphasis

By stressing too many words in your prose, you run the risk of treating your readers like children who need to be told how to read.

Imagine you are an actor given this dialogue by an over-eager playwright:

> **BILL:** (angrily) I won't take this anymore. I've had enough of you and John. You've ruined my life. (questioningly) Margery? Are you listening to me?

(quietly) I'm going to pack my things and get the hell out of here. (whispering) I love you.

Your thoughts? It is obvious the playwright has no confidence in the actor's ability to interpret the text, and feels that extra emphasis is needed to point him/her in the right direction. The actor would not be impressed. He may also doubt the quality of the playwright. I certainly would.

Let's take a look at the above in prose form:

> "I won't *take* this anymore," said Bill. "I've *had* enough of you and John. You've *ruined* my life. Margery? Are you *listening* to me? I'm going to pack my things and get the *hell* out of here. I *love* you."

Do we need any of the above emphasis?

No, we don't.

The reader is intelligent. They get what is going on by reading the words on the page. They do not need your direction to interpret how Bill is speaking.

And, as a further layer to this, it may be possible that the reader's *inner Bill* - Bill's voice as heard in their mind - has a different emphasis and flow:

> *"I* won't take this *anymore,"* said Bill. *"I've* had enough of you and John. *You've* ruined my life. Margery? Are *you* listening to me? I'm going to *pack* my things and get the hell out of here. *I* love you."

By adding too much emphasis, the flow of your sentences may jar with the reader.

I have used dialogue as my example, but the advice is also for prose: use emphasis sparingly, if at all.

Don't quote me
When defining or referencing a phrase or quotation, it needs quotation marks NOT italics.

> **Example (using both American and British styles):**
> **US:** "John told me, 'Go home, pack all your things and meet me at the canal boat,' but he didn't turn up," said Margery.
>
> **UK:** 'John told me, "Go home, pack all your things and meet me at the canal boat," but he didn't turn up,' said Margery.

It's my first time… be gentle
When introducing an unfamiliar phrase to the reader (most usually in non-fiction) use single quotation marks.

> **Example:**
> "We will find Bill using a 'conceptual map' of the area," said the esoteric policeman.
>
> **Later:**
> John examined the conceptual map and was perplexed.

Once you have introduced the new phrase, you do not need

to use quotations again.

I'm not scared!

A 'scare quote' or, as it is sometimes called, a 'sneer quote' is used when the author/writer (or a character) does not agree with the use of the word in its present context and emphasises it with the use of double quotations.

Examples:

"John is one "cool" guy," said Bill.

This indicates that Bill doesn't think John is cool. He is showing a sense of disdain - he means the *opposite of cool.*

If you use double quotation marks to emphasise words, you run the risk of creating an unwanted sneer quote.

Example:

Your good health is "guaranteed" at John's Health Spa.

With this statement, injury seems the most likely outcome!

As you can see, a slight change in the way you use quotation marks can have a serious impact on your intended meaning.

Make sure you use them wisely.

Oh, one more thing - if you liked this section, please quote me...

EDIT: #28

Search your novel for quotation marks.

Are they used correctly? Replace single quotations for italics whenever possible.

EDIT: #29

Skim read your novel for emphasising italics.

Consider every instance of italics. Are they needed? Are they used correctly?

Remember: Do not over-emphasise

ii. Planes, Trains & Automobiles

…and books, magazines, movies, TV shows and plays. When do we capitalise and when do we italicise?

What's the title of your novel, Kev?
Thanks for asking. I'm calling it, *All About Copywriting.*

Titles of works creates a lot of confusion in the complex world of italics and capitalisation. Here is a quick guide:

Books, eBooks, booklets
Magazine
Newspapers
Journals

Titles of all the above should use italics.

For books, ALL the title is italicised:

> *The Lord of the Rings*
> *The Indie Editor*
> *The Catcher in the Rye*

For magazines and newspapers, be careful to notice that 'the' is not italicised:

> The *Sunday Times*
> *Cosmopolitan*
> The *Wall Street Journal*

Articles from magazines and newspapers and individual sections in books are not italicised, but instead use double quotation marks:

> "Concerning Hobbits"
> "Something that I said?"
> "The Boy Who Lived"
> "A Day in the Life of a Paramedic"
> "Another Week, Another Murder"

Movies
Television Shows
Plays
Musical Works

All should be italicised:

> *Star Wars: The Force Awakens*
> *Red Dwarf*
> *A Streetcar Named Desire*
> *The Dark Side of the Moon*

Individual episodes of television shows or songs from an album are not italicised, but instead use quotation marks:

> *Red Dwarf* - "Gunmen of the Apocalypse"
> The Dark Side of the Moon - *"Us and Them"*

Ships
Planes
Trains

All should be italicised:

The Millennium Falcon
Lancaster Bomber
The Flying Scotsman

Websites
Websites are not italicised and not put in quotation marks.
They are capitalised as in headline form.

Examples:
Facebook
Wikipedia
Windows Live
Google

It's my trade
Branded names are neither italicised nor written in
quotation marks. They are all capitalised.

Examples:
Ford
Disney
Apple
Blue Sky Studios

It takes a while to get the hang of these conventions, but it
is well worth your while to learn them - you never know

when they will come in handy.

EDIT: #30

Search your novel for titles of publications, websites, music, TV shows, brand names, etc.
Apply the correct formatting.

iii. Foreign Words, Sounds & Letters

Yes, more things to italicise!

It's foreign to me
Always italicise foreign words. But hang on, the English language is littered with foreign words. Some of them, like *bungalow, jungle* or *croissant,* are now a part of this extensive language (English is five times larger than any other language).

Do I italicise them all?

No.

The rule of thumb is to italicise the foreign words your readers are not likely to know. If your word appears in the dictionary, it's considered *common* and should not be italicised.

If the words form a long sentence, do not italicise but put the whole sentence in quotation marks.

A box full of letters
When you are referencing a letter, *Z,* for instance, always italicise.

Examples:
When attempting to burn down John's shed, Bill followed his meticulous plan from *A* to *Z.*

Sounds good

For sounds reproduced as words, the convention is to italicise them, but you won't lose any marks if you don't.

Examples:
Brrr
Aaaargh
Thwack
Bang

And that, is the end of the confusing world of italics, but don't breathe just yet - coming up next - more capitalisation rules. Yay!

EDIT: #31

Search your novel for foreign words, letters of the alphabet and sounds.
Apply the correct formatting.

iv. Family Names & Titles

Knowing what and when to capitalise can be a problem. I'm assuming you know your basic rules, so let's look at a few areas of confusion.

What about my mum & dad?
The simple rule is to capitalise when the *family name* is replacing the *real name*.

Example:
Steve chatted to Claire about Bill's marital problems.

If Steve and Claire are *mum and dad* and Bill *the uncle,* then we can rewrite the sentence:

Dad chatted to Mum about Uncle Bill's marital problems.

Let's try an example of the opposite case:
Every mum loves flowers on her birthday.

Mum is not capitalised, because *mum* can be replaced by *girl* or *woman* but not by *Claire* or any other name.

(By the way, I'm not suggesting all women like flowers; I'm just using this as an example).

What's in a title?
Titles are capitalised in the same way as family members.

Examples:

At the helm of his narrow boat, <u>Captain</u> John guided the craft into its moorings.

The <u>captain</u> saluted Bill and Margery and invited them on board.

In the second sentence, we cannot change captain to John, so captain does not use a capital.

Once you know this simple rule, it is easy to navigate through your writing and correct any mistakes.

EDIT: #32

Search your novel for titles and family names like <u>mum</u>, <u>dad</u>, <u>uncle</u>, <u>aunt</u>, <u>father</u>, <u>mother</u>, etc.
Use the correct capitalisation.

v. Directions

Why are directions sometimes capitalised and at other times not? The answer is straightforward - *sort of.*

A sense of direction
The simple rule is this:

> If you are *naming* a region, use upper case
> If *describing* a direction, use lowercase.

Examples:
John was proud to be from the <u>North</u> whilst Bill was thrilled to be from the <u>South</u>.

Margery often wondered what was so boring about <u>east</u> and <u>west</u>.

John came from <u>Northern</u> Ireland, Bill grew up on the <u>South</u> Downs.

John's shed sat in the <u>south-west</u> corner of his garden. Bill's statue of Aphrodite pointed to the <u>North</u>.

Confusion comes with terms like <u>northerner</u>. Do we capitalise or not? Both are acceptable:

John is a <u>northerner</u>, Bill is a <u>Southerner</u>.

However, we cannot use both instances in our sentence, nor in our fiction. Your novel needs to be consistent. Choose a style and stick to it.

John is a <u>northerner</u>, Bill is a <u>southerner</u>.

Hope you didn't get lost...

EDIT: #33
Search your novel for <u>north</u>, <u>south</u>, <u>east</u> and <u>west</u>.
If a directional term is a compass point use lowercase. If it is a region, then capitalise.
Remember: Be consistent.

vi. Numbers, Dates & Time

There are no set rules, but there a few conventions. Whichever way you decide to tackle numbers, do so consistently.

I've got your number
The generally accepted convention *suggests,* whenever possible, to use words for numbers between 0-100.

> **Examples (notice how compound numbers are joined by a hyphen):**
>
> John viewed Margery as his <u>thirty-seventh</u> conquest.
>
> Margery waited <u>twenty-five</u> minutes before leaving the house.
>
> Margery gave Bill <u>one</u> more chance.
>
> Bill counted <u>127</u> reasons why Margery should stay.

Why do we use this convention between 0-100? Because sometimes spelling out complex numbers is impractical:

> **Which is easier to read?**
> Bill sent Margery five-thousand, two-hundred and thirty-one letters over the time of their marriage.
>
> Bill sent Margery 5,231 letters over the time of their marriage.

Quite clearly, the second sentence is easier on the eye (and the brain) than the first.

Consider these examples:

Margery gave Bill 1 more chance.

John viewed Margery as his 37th conquest.

Margery waited 25 minutes before leaving the house.

All the above examples are considered against the numbering convention, but are acceptable as long as you are consistent. But be aware this will jar with some readers (myself included).

What about large numbers like 10,000 or 60,000,000?
They are written like this:

Ten thousand
Sixty million

The conventions, as you can now probably guess, are all about making numbers easy to read. Sixty million is easier to read than 60,000,000.

Generally, it is best not to mix numbers and words in the same sentence:

Bill wrote to Margery three times a day over seven years - exactly 5,321 letters.

Bill wrote to Margery 3 times a day over 7 years - exactly 5,321 letters.

Again, this is the convention because the second sentence is easier to read.

What if we have two numbers directly next to each other in the same sentence?

Consider these two examples:
Bill stole 25 six-inch nails from John's shed.
Bill stole 25 6-inch nails from John's shed.

Clearly, the top example is easier to read. In this situation, mixing words and numbers is acceptable and desirable.

What about starting sentences with numbers?

157 texts arrived for Margery in one month.

Yes, it's awkward. In this situation, the convention is to write the numbers out in full:

One hundred and fifty-seven texts arrived for Margery in one month.

Fractions?
Spell them out and hyphenate them.

Margery withdrew exactly <u>four-fifths</u> of their savings.

John was <u>two-thirds</u> in love with Margery. The last

niggling <u>one-third</u> caused all the problems.

And decimals?

Always use the numerical version for decimals unless they can be replaced by a quarter, half, third, fifth, etc.

The nearest star to Earth is Proxima Centuari at a whopping <u>4.22</u> light years distance.

The average age of the solar system is <u>four and a half billion</u> years old.

Symbols?

They are not exactly numbers, but the convention is to write them: <u>per cent</u>, <u>number</u>, <u>pounds</u>, <u>feet</u>, <u>inches</u>, etc.

It's a date!

Writing dates is more about consistency and ease of reading. And, of course, your personal style.

Examples:

John's Birthday is the 27th March, thought Margery.

Bill first met Margery on the twenty-second of December.

Both the above examples are acceptable, but the general belief is words are better than numbers, particularly in dialogue.

Date ranges:

John was away between the twenty-fifth of March and the second of April.

Decades

Both words and numbers are acceptable.

All the below are satisfactory examples:

Bill met Margery in the <u>nineties</u>.

The <u>mid-1990s</u> were a time of discovery for Margery.

John bought his boat in the late '90s - the last few years of the <u>twentieth century</u>.

A common error to watch out for (and one that can lead editors, reviewers and, worst of all: other authors, perceiving you as an incompetent writer) is to include an unnecessary apostrophe:

1990's
The 70's

They are plurals and do not need an apostrophe.

Get these right.

Making the time up

Always use numerals in conjunction with <u>a.m.</u> & <u>p.m.</u>

First things first.

How do we write a.m. and p.m.?
a.m.
p.m.

Always put a space between the numbers and a.m. or p.m. and a colon between the hours and the minutes:

7:15 a.m.
9:27 p.m.

6:25 a.m. or six twenty-five a.m.?
If you want to use words instead of numerals you must drop the a.m. or p.m.

Correct examples:
6:25 a.m.
Six twenty-five in the morning.

Incorrect examples:
6:25 in the morning.
Six twenty-five a.m.

Do not put a hyphen between hours and minutes:

Incorrect: Six-twenty-five.

Correct: Six twenty-five.

How to use *o'clock*

Example:
"I'm meeting John at nine o'clock this evening," said Margery.

If we are referring to parts of hours, then we can generally drop the o'clock altogether:

I am meeting Bill at nine o'clock and John at ten thirty.

Following the above conventions will make reading of your fiction smoother and give your novel consistency.

EDIT: #34

Search your novel for numerals and written numbers.
Apply the conventions at your own discretion. Make sure they are consistent.
Do not put unnecessary apostrophes in decades!

SECTION FIVE
Speech

Handling dialogue in fiction can be problematic. This section looks at how to avoid some of the more common pitfalls and examines ways to make your conversations more readable.

In this section:

i. He Said/She Said
Dialogue in modern fiction 123

ii. Exclamation Marks
When to use them! And!! Overuse!! 124

iii. Ellipsis...
All about those three little dots 133

i. He Said/She Said

This section is not so much about bad writing as about *writing style* and concerns ways to tackle dialogue in modern fiction.

It will not tell you when to use dialogue, but advise on how to handle it between your characters.

The genre of your novel will dictate pace and style, but it is important to recognise that contemporary fiction usually avoids long pieces of narrative and stodgy dialogue handling.

Modern readers want things *to move*.

The he said/she said techniques I am outlining here are suggestions only; your emphasis must be on consistency.

If you are happy with your handling of dialogue, you may want to skip this section. Otherwise, read on.

Say what?

> **Consider these:**
> "I hate you!" said Bill.
> "Why, Bill? What have I done?" said Margery.
> "John told me everything," said Bill.
> "But he promised to keep it a secret," said Margery.
> "John promised lots of things," said Bill.
> "I don't care. I love him," said Margery.

The exchange makes sense, but all those <u>saids</u> are a little clunky. We might consider swapping them for *shouted* or *replied* etc.:

> "I hate you!" <u>shouted</u> Bill.
> "Why, Bill? What have I done?" <u>replied</u> Margery.
> "John told me everything," <u>continued</u> Bill.
> "But he promised to keep it a secret," <u>whispered</u> Margery.
> "John promised lots of things," said Bill.
> "I don't care. I love him," said Margery.

The dialogue is more readable but still clunky. We can do better.

> **Let's make a further, stylistic change and place some of the <u>saids</u> before the dialogue:**
> Bill shouted, "I hate you!"
> "Why, Bill? What have I done?" replied Margery.
> "John told me everything," continued Bill.
> Margery whispered, "But he promised to keep it a secret."
> "John promised lots of things," said Bill.
> "I don't care. I love him," said Margery.

The above examples are acceptable ways of portraying dialogue in fiction. However, in some quarters, using he <u>said/she</u> said is seen as *old fashioned* and distracting from the action.

The technique has its supporters and it is true to say that after a while, the <u>saids</u> *become invisible,* but I find too many saids and replieds off-putting. In my opinion, the technique smacks of Lazy Writing.

This is just my opinion - there are no set rules.

Bring in the new
Let's tackle the above dialogue using a more modern technique.

The first line...
"I hate you!" said/shouted Bill.

...is straightforward, the meaning is clear.

Can we improve on it? ...I think we can.

Consider:
Bill thumped the table. "I hate you!"

The meaning is the same, yet we have lost 'said Bill' and, as a bonus, we've added some action, some *show not tell*. The reader knows it's Bill speaking because he thumped the table. Combine this with an exclamation mark and the reader doesn't need to be told Bill is shouting.

Exclamation marks signify intensity of emotion and loud outbursts and sounds - its presence is enough to convey how Bill is speaking.

This technique is useful for exclusive dialogue between two characters. Once the order of speech has been established, the saids can be dropped from the rest of the dialogue:

> Bill thumped the table. "I hate you!"
> Margery jumped. "Why Bill? What have I done?"
> "John told me everything."
> "But he promised to keep it a secret."
> "John promised lots of things."
> "I don't care. I love him."

No <u>saids</u> are needed to tell us who is speaking. And if we do feel the need to remind our reader, we use action:

> Bill thumped the table. "I hate you!"
> Margery jumped. "Why Bill? What have I done?"
> "John told me everything."
> "But he promised to keep it a secret."
> "John promised lots of things."
> Margery collapsed onto the bed, burying her face in a pillow. "I don't care. I love him."

Already the dialogue is more compelling - and not a <u>said</u> in sight.

Don't all speak at once

The above technique works for two-person conversations, but what about dialogue between multiple characters?

The reader must always know who is speaking. If you need to use a <u>said</u> for clarity, this outweighs all other concerns. This technique does not recommend removing them all - but instead argues for an emphasis on *action* in dialogue.

There is an argument that says readers should know who is talking just by the way the character is written -

making <u>saids</u> redundant - but not all characters can have immediately recognisable speech patterns - and these are hard to maintain in urgent conversations.

The most important thing to remember is *clarity*. The reader comes first.

N.B. No <u>saids</u> were harmed in the making of this section.

EDIT: #35

Search your novel for dialogue.

Aim to minimise <u>saids</u> in dialogue by replacing them with *action* whenever you can. Do not stop using them for the sake of it.

Remember: Do not sacrifice clarity for style. Keep dialogue and characters consistent.

ii. Exclamation Marks

We all sometimes guilty of overusing the excitable exclamation mark!!!

Why?!
Because we are eager to express as much emotion on the page as possible!

The downside!? Yeah, it makes us look amateurish and childlike! And what is all the shouting about?!

No!!!!!!!!!

What is an exclamation mark for?
They are used to convey volume, intensity and exuberance.

Is that it?

Yes, that's it. You shouldn't be using it for anything else.

So using exclamations is good, yes?
In moderation? …A hesitant *yes*.

Let's revisit *show not tell* for a moment. Using an exclamation mark can sometimes support Lazy Writing by *telling* us an emotion and not *showing* it to us.

Example:
"I am shocked!" shouted Bill.

A horrible generic statement. Let's remove the exclamation

and see what happens:

"I am shocked," shouted Bill.

We have the same sentence and no exclamation. If you feel the sentence is shouting out for an exclamation, it may because you overuse them - I'd even go as far as saying there is no *may* about it. Whatever you might think, the second example is acceptable dialogue in fiction.

Still not convinced, yet feel the need to cut down on your exclamation use? Then *action* can save the day:

The news hit Bill with the full force of a ten-ton truck. He fell, slack-jawed, onto the sofa, his eyes jack-knifing between the floor and Margery's tear-stained face.

Okay, I went a little overboard, but the action speaks for itself - and no exclamation mark in sight.

Result!

Let's take a look at another example:
"You cannot leave me!" Bill shouted.
"But I must!" said Margery. "I must!"
"I won't let you!"
"I love John!"
"Don't say that!"

The exclamation mark expresses one level of intensity. The above scene has no highs, no lows. The conversation sounds like an exchange from TV soap - melodramatic and shouty. Where is the finesse?

Are your readers to assume that the narrator and/or characters are in a perpetual state of shock?

The law of diminishing returns?
Think of it like this: Every single exclamation mark reduces the power and effect of those exclamation marks that come after it.

How many is too many?
The average modern novel is 300-350 pages long (50-75,000 words). You should aim for one exclamation mark every three pages maximum, but bear in mind this is 116 exclamations in an entire novel.

116!

How many exclamations are in your novel?

Social media explosion!
A distinction needs to be drawn between the recent proliferation of exclamation marks in emails, status updates, texting and modern fiction.

It is more than acceptable to use exclamation marks in these new areas (and fun). However, that does not mean the same can be said for your fiction.

Writing trends are always moving. At the moment, you cannot and should not use exclamations in the same way you do with social media. To do so is viewed as Bad Writing.

OMG!

EDIT: #36

Search your novel for exclamation marks with particular attention to your first ten pages.

Remove and rewrite. *Show* the reader the shock and intensity. Do not always *tell* them.

Remember: In this instance, less definitely is more!!!!

iii. Ellipsis...

What is an ellipsis? A punctuation mark consisting of three dots/full-stops/periods in a row, like at the end of this sentence...

Writers tend to use the ellipsis for:
Unfinished sentences/trailing off
Hesitation
Pause
Missing text

Let's look at the ellipsis in action.

Trailing off:
"I can't believe you're going to stay..." Bill's voice faltered.

Hesitation:
"...I can't believe you're going."

Pause:
"I can't believe you're...leaving me."
Bill was sick of Margery and John...of everything.

Missing text:
"You can't be leaving me for...I don't believe it."

The ellipsis is used to add:
Emphasis
Mystery
Complication

Momentum
Confusion
Uneasiness

Lazy writers often use the ellipsis to try to create tension. It should never be used for this purpose. If you can't get the tension across through your words, then you won't do it with an ellipsis.

Something is missing

The ellipsis can also be used to indicate the omission of words in the middle of quoted sentences - let's look at an excerpt from the newspaper article about Bill's shed burning behaviour:

> "A middle-aged man and amateur sculptor, Bill Watkins, was charged yesterday for trespass and wilful damage to the property of his neighbour, John McGinty. During the early hours of Thursday morning, Mr Watkins forced his way into Mr McGinty's garden and set fire to a shed before his arrest by police. The attack was part of a long-running feud involving Mr Watkins' wife."

Now let's quote it, using the ellipsis to cherry-pick the meat of the story:

> "A middle-aged man ... Bill Watkins, was charged yesterday for trespass and wilful damage to the property of his neighbour, John McGinty ... Mr Watkins ... set fire to a shed before his arrest by police ... part of a long-running feud involving Mr Watkins' wife."

The ellipsis allows for a précis of the action without the extra baggage.

Overuse...of...the...ellipsis...

The Internet, like with the Exclamation Mark, has led to a proliferation of the ellipsis in emails and social media. As such, it has also found its way, more and more, into modern fiction.

I certainly overuse it. And find myself defending its use when I know there are other tools at my disposal like commas and semi-colons. But as much as I adore those enigmatic three dots, I still - in the cold, hard light of day - edit them out.

EDIT: #37

Search your novel for the ellipsis.
Remove and rewrite. Add pauses by using commas and semi-colons.

SECTION SIX
Tricky Words

In this section:

i. Single Word Modifiers of Doom
Quite useful, very informative, really helpful 139

ii. However & Nevertheless / Moreover
& Furthermore
How to avoid sounding like an essay 141

iii. Little Words Causing Big Trouble
So it even began to seem quite useful already 143

iv. As
Don't mess with the sequence 155

v. Circumlocutions
*At this point in time, in the near future and
in light of the fact* 159

i. Single Word Modifiers of Doom

What words qualify to make it to this list? Let's take a look:

Very
Really
Quite
Actually
Already
Fairly
Much
Totally
Only
Almost/Mostly/Most
Nearly

The question asked of these words is:
Do they do anything?

The answer:
No. They are mostly unnecessary and frequently redundant.

Examples:

John was <u>very</u> pleased with his <u>totally</u> successful chat-up line.

It was <u>quite</u> late and Margery was <u>really</u> <u>very</u> tired.

Let's remove those unwanted words:

John was pleased with his successful chat-up line.

It was later than expected and Margery was exhausted.

You will notice that some of these words cropped up in Section One - "Adverbs, Adjectives & Only". Hopefully, you found most of these little blighters and they are already eradicated, if not, you know what to do.

EDIT: #38

Search your novel for single word modifiers:

Very

Really

Quite

Actually

Fairly

Much

Totally

Only

Almost

Nearly

Do they add anything to the sentence? If not - remove.

ii. However & Nevertheless
Moreover & Furthermore

Hang on Kev, I'm pretty sure you've used *however* in this guide (twenty-six times, because I just counted).

True, but this is non-fiction and I'm using an informal narrative - which pretty much allows me to get away with anything I want writing-wise, *however,* let's not get bogged down in this discussion.

Proper Usage
However and nevertheless are normally placed at the beginning of a sentence when contrasting two ideas.

Nevertheless is seen as *formal.*

However is seen as *less formal*

Examples:
"Margery is not coming home for a while. However, she has agreed to phone me once a week to try and talk our way through this."

Bill returned from the Police Station feeling like a hero. Nevertheless, the residents of the tight-knit cul-de-sac treated him as an outcast.

This usage is not wrong per se, but the terms are more suited to a non-fiction guide or an essay than to modern fiction.

Consider replacing however and nevertheless with:

Even so

In spite of / In spite of this

Yet he/she/they still

Moreover & furthermore

A common writing mistake is to confuse the usage of moreover and furthermore, with that of however and nevertheless.

However and nevertheless mean: *in spite of.*

Moreover and furthermore mean: *in addition to.*

Regardless of this difference, try to eradicate these terms from your writing. Of course, you might have a professor character who talks like an essay - that would be fine - but for prose, you want to remove most instances.

EDIT: #39

Search your novel for however and nevertheless, moreover and furthermore.

Remove and rewrite most instances.

iii. Little Words Causing Big Trouble

This section deals with <u>little</u>, <u>got</u>, <u>even</u>, <u>so</u>, <u>a lot</u>, <u>of</u> and <u>seemed/began</u>.

Got

We have good words, we have bad words and sometimes we have words that are just plain ugly.

What have I got against got?

It is a poor, lazy, uncouth verb.

Let's look at got in action:

Bill got up and found Margery's note.

Got up is a common spoken phrase, but in written form, it jars.

Let's fix it:

Bill awoke to find Margery's note.

Sometimes <u>got</u> is used to replace a helping verb like have:

"I <u>got</u> a captain's hat," said John.

See how John now sounds like he's three years old? And because <u>got</u> is a weak verb, the meaning is not clear.

Did John *have, find* or even *steal* the hat?

Possibly…

The English language is stuffed with other far more powerful verbs than <u>got</u> - if this word crops up in your fiction, I suggest you use them.

EDIT: #40
Search your novel for <u>got</u>.
Remove, replace, rewrite.
Remember: If used in dialogue you may wish to keep it.

Even

This is another unnecessary adjective. It sits in sentences looking all cool and pleased with itself, but the reality? <u>Even</u> can be mostly removed without consequence.

Example:
Bill wasn't <u>even</u> aware of Margery staring at him.

<u>Even</u> Bill agreed with Margery - John looked fashonable in a captain's hat.

Margery <u>even</u> clapped her hands together when John spoke.

Now let's delete those <u>evens</u>:

Bill wasn't aware of Margery staring at him.

Bill agreed with Margery - John looked fashionable in a captain's hat.

Margery clapped her hands together when John spoke.

The use of <u>even</u> can add an unnecessary jarring emphasis. However, there are instances where it is acceptable:

John was an <u>even</u> better raconteur than Old Dave, the pub's resident story-teller.

The <u>even</u> is tolerable, but I'd still consider removing it.

EDIT: #41

Search your novel for <u>even</u>.

Consider each and every usage. If unnecessary, remove, replace, rewrite.

Remember: If used in dialogue you may wish to keep it.

So

A vague intensifier adding weak emphasis to adjectives.

Example:
Bill was <u>so</u> peeved with John.

The result of using <u>so</u> is negligible. *Peeved* is a strong enough word without adding such a weak modifier:

Bill was peeved with John.

The meaning is no less enhanced.

However, if <u>so</u> is paired with an action it becomes stronger:

Bill was so peeved with John that he set fire to his shed.

This second instance is more acceptable.

So what?
For a start off, <u>so</u> is a word used a routinely in every day speech. It is used in a similar way to the word 'like' - insomuch that it can represent a pause.

Example:
Margery sat with John. They shared, *like,* a beautiful moment, *like.* Two people in love, *like,* oblivious to the world.

Let's write the same sentence using so, to see what I mean:

> So Margery sat with John. They so shared a beautiful moment. Two people so much in love, so oblivious to the world.

As we can see, so is mostly not needed. Let's fix it:

> Margery sat with John. They shared a beautiful moment. Two people so in love, oblivious to the world.

So can easily slip into your sentences.

It can be useful to add emphasis, but over usage will make your prose flabby and will jar with the reader.

So to speak
I've read fiction where both the protagonists start the majority of their conversations with so.

This is a common habit to fall into.

> **Examples:**

> "So what you're telling me is, Margery likes John?"

> "So Bill set fire to the shed?"

> "So your husband has a criminal record?"

So is nothing more than an unwanted pause.

The fix is a simple one:

"You're telling me Margery likes John?"

"Bill set fire to the shed?"

"Your husband has a criminal record?"

By removing so we create better flowing, more direct sentences.

So too clarify please
Sometimes writers fall into the habit of using so instead of the word 'too' and other words like 'please'.

Examples:
Bill didn't feel so good.
"So understand this is nothing personal."

At first glance they appear to be all right, but in both cases so is the incorrect word.

Let's fix the above examples:
Bill didn't feel *too* good.
"Please understand this is nothing personal.

Using so in colloquial speech is acceptable, but overusing it will make your writing sloppy.

The pauses will jar with the reader.

EDIT: #42

Search your novel for <u>so</u>.

Remove, replace, rewrite

Remember: If used in dialogue you may wish to keep it.

A Lot

Let's quantify <u>a lot</u>. How much exactly is <u>a lot</u>? Is <u>a lot</u>, <u>a lot</u> more or <u>a lot</u> less than quite <u>a lot</u>?

Can you see the problem?

Using <u>a lot</u> means nothing. Eliminate <u>a lot</u> from your manuscript and you will eliminate <u>a lot</u> of problems - I'm just not sure how many...

Be aware that <u>a lot</u> is commonly misspelled as <u>alot</u>.

> **Example:**
> Bill was in <u>a lot</u> of trouble; he had <u>a lot</u> of explaining to do.

> **The fix:**
> Bill was sinking into quicksand. How was he going to talk his way out of this?

EDIT: #43

Search your novel for <u>a lot</u>/<u>alot</u>.
Remove, replace, rewrite
Remember: If used in dialogue you may wish to keep it.

Almost/Seemed/Began/Started

Does the action in your story only <u>seem</u> to be happening? Or is your action only <u>beginning</u> to happen?

Examples:

Bill <u>began</u> to get annoyed.

John <u>started</u> to speak.

Margery was <u>almost</u> afraid.

Bill <u>seemed</u> upset.

Margery <u>began</u> to sob.

All this shilly-shallying around gets us nowhere.

Write with authority:

Bill was annoyed.

John spoke.

Margery was afraid.

Bill was upset.

Margery sobbed.

We've removed all the <u>begans</u> and <u>almosts</u> etc. without losing the meaning. The writing is more direct.

You might also consider rewriting with more action rather than just removing the offending words.

Consider this sentence:
Bill found the situation <u>almost</u> unbearable.

Can we change the sentence without losing the meaning? No. Bill is suffering, but surviving. However, this is lazy writing. Why not try:

Bill lived on the raw edge of a nervous breakdown.

Or:

Long anxious days followed sleepless nights. A daily torture from which there was no escape. But Bill endured.

The moment has a crescendo. When things are <u>seeming</u> or <u>starting</u>, we miss the bang and end up with a whimper. Be aware of how certain modifiers can dampen the moment.

EDIT: #44
Search your novel for <u>almost</u>/<u>seemed</u>/<u>began</u>/<u>started</u>. Replace with authority.

iv. As

How come as isn't in the "Little Words Causing Big Trouble" section of this section? This is because there is more to as than meets the eye. The misuse and overuse of as can negatively affect how your writing is perceived.

What, when, how?
Events in the real world can all happen at the same time, but events in fiction happen sequentially.

Why?

Because readers prefer to read sequentially - a principal you should apply to all your fiction.

Using as has a negative effect on your action. If you want to come across as an accomplished writer - remove them.

Still not convinced?

Example:
John put his arm around Margery as Bill entered the garden.

We know that Bill can enter the garden at the same time that John is putting his arm around Margery, but the events need to be described sequentially so the reader can make sense of the action:

Bill entered the garden. John put his arm around Margery.

Creating a sequence of events is easier for the reader and - frankly - less clunky.

Another Example:
Bill grimaced <u>as</u> John put his arm around Margery.

The above is a common error. At first glance it appears all is well and fine - but let's take a closer look at the example with reference to cause-and-effect.

What is the cause?
John putting his arm around Margery.

What is the effect?
Bill grimacing.

Both cannot happen simultaneously as the example suggests. John must put his arm around Margery before Bill can react with his grimace.

The fix? Let's try two solutions:

John put his arm around Margery. Bill grimaced.

Bill grimaced because John put his arm around Margery.

Using <u>as</u> is acceptable, but if you overuse this connecting word (as some authors have a habit of doing), your prose will suffer.

Abandon <u>as</u> whenever possible in this context and, instead, create a sequence of events. Your readers will thank you for it.

You know what they say:
Time Travel! What do we want? NOW! When do we want it?

EDIT: #45
Search your novel for <u>as</u>.
Is <u>as</u> necessary? If not, rewrite, creating a series of events with emphasis on cause and effect.
Remember: In real life, things don't always happen for a reason. In fiction, they do. Kick your <u>as</u> goodbye.

v. Circumlocutions

Circumlo-what? A circumlocution is a set of words which don't really mean anything or which can be used in evasive speaking.

Come again?

Example:
There is no doubt that.

…is a circuitous way of saying:

Doubtless.

Another example:
An efficient tool for cutting and collecting grass.

…is:

A lawn-mower.

You getting it now?

Let's look at a series of common circumlocutions and their meaning:

It is necessary/possible that - May, might, could
He is a man who - He
In a hasty manner - Hastily
At this point in time - Now
In the near future - Soon

In light of the fact - Because
Prior to, in anticipation of, following on, at the same time as - Before, after, as
Notwithstanding the fact that, despite the fact that - Although
Concerning the matter of - About
The reason for, owing to the reason that, on the grounds that - Because, since, why
If it should transpire that, in the event that - If
With regard to - About
Owing to the fact that, due to the fact that, in view of the fact that - Since, because
This is a subject which - This subject
In a situation in which - When
Is able to, has the capacity to - Can
There is the possibility - May, might, could
On the occasion of - When
For the purpose of - To
The question as to whether - Whether

Going around in circles

No-one is immune to the above examples of verbosity and whilst it is possible to allow your characters to use circumlocutions, I would suggest keeping them to a minimum within your prose.

If you are like me, you'll probably overuse your own circumlocutions.

Become aware of them and add to the above list.

EDIT: #46

Search your novel for circumlocutions.

Use less verbosity where appropriate. Replace with fewer, targeted words.

Remember: Talking about circumlocutions with your friends can make you sound intelligent and witty. Using too many in your novel will have the opposite effect.

SECTION SEVEN
Pairs & Homonyms

Yes, it's all those pesky little word combinations sent to earth to drive us all crazy.

In this section:

i. Effect/Affect
How to use this effect and not let it affect you 165

ii. Who/Whom
To whomever it may concern....................................167

iii. All Right/Alright
Do the right thing...169

iv. On To/Onto
Hold on! 171

v. In To / Into
Getting into it! 173

vi. Homophones
*If you no won thing, no this: don't let
you're self get throne* 175

i. Effect/Affect

Do you find it difficult knowing when to use <u>effective</u> and <u>affective</u>? Let's try and clarify the problem.

Effect?
We use <u>effect</u> when talking about the ending or result of a consequence.

<u>Effect</u> signifies change caused by something:

Johns honest intentions were simple and <u>effective</u>.

Bill's letters had no <u>effect</u> on Margery.

Affect?
We use <u>affect</u> when talking about an influence.

<u>Affect</u> signifies influence but no change:

Bill's letter <u>affected</u> Margery. She thought about his words all day.

John's speech was <u>affective</u>.

In a nutshell: When you <u>affect</u> something, you create an <u>effect</u> on it (<u>effect</u> is a noun; <u>affect</u> is a verb).

EDIT: #47
Search your novel for <u>affect</u>/<u>effect</u>.
Check the words are used correctly and fix.

ii. Who/Whom

There is an easy way of knowing when to use <u>who</u> or <u>whom</u>.

Let's look at this sentence:
Bill stared at John - the man <u>who/whom</u> he hated more than anyone else.

Is it who or whom?

Here is how you can find out. We simply substitute he/she for <u>who</u> and him/her for <u>whom</u>.

If he or she is the correct form, the proper choice is <u>who</u>.

If him or her is the correct form, use <u>whom</u>.

Let's try the sentence again using this technique:

Bill stared at John - the man <u>whom</u> he hated more than anyone else. (Bill hates *him* more than anyone else - so we choose <u>whom</u>.)

More examples:
<u>Who</u> is that man in the garden? *(He* is in the garden - so we choose <u>who</u>).

John is the man <u>whom</u> Margery went boating with last week. (Margery went boating with *him* - we choose whom)

John is the guy <u>who</u> got the girl. (*He* got the girl - so we choose who)

Subject/Object

In all the above examples we are making a distinction between subject and object.

For subject *(he/she)* we choose <u>who</u>.

For object *(him/her)* we chose <u>whom</u>.

Easy...

Regarding modern writing

As <u>whom</u> is dropped in modern speech patterns in favour of <u>who</u>, its misuse is acceptable in dialogue. You might also decide to do the same for prose – if so, be consistent.

EDIT: #48

Search your novel for <u>who</u>/<u>whom</u>.
Check for correct use and fix.
Remember: Be consistent.

iii. All Right/Alright.

I'll be honest, I prefer <u>alright</u> and always have done. Other merged words such as 'altogether' are standard in English and it won't be long before <u>alright</u> joins them down the pub for a well-earned merged-word drink. But in the meantime there is an issue.

Should I use <u>alright</u> in my fiction?

Yes and no.

<u>All right</u> always looks wrong to me, but I know that not everyone shares this viewpoint and, until <u>alright</u> is accepted as Standard English, I will continue to use the older term.

A simple approach
For prose use <u>all right</u>. For dialogue, use <u>alright</u>. You may disagree, just make sure your usage is consistent.

EDIT: #49
Search your novel for all <u>right</u>/<u>alright</u>.
Make changes where necessary.
Remember: Be consistent.

iv. On To/Onto

The on to/onto divide spans the Atlantic. Writers in the USA tend towards onto, whereas in Britain, on to is favoured.

Onto has been around since the Nineteenth Century and is an informal contraction. Its usage is becoming more and more common.

Not everyone accepts onto as part of the English language, particularly in formal writing. However, it is acceptable in fiction.

You must make sure you use it properly and consistently.

Correct usage:

Bill threw John onto the grass.

Margery clambered onto John's boat

Incorrect usage:

Margery went onto list many reasons why Bill must change.

Margery left Bill and moved onto a new life with John.

On to should never be written as a single word if it means 'onwards' or 'towards'.

Let's fix those incorrect sentences:

Margery went <u>on</u> <u>to</u> list many reasons why Bill must change.

Margery left Bill and moved <u>on</u> <u>to</u> a new life with John.

EDIT: #50

Search for <u>onto</u> and <u>on</u> <u>to</u>.

Make sure they are used correctly.

Remember: <u>On</u> <u>to</u> should never be written as a single word if it means 'onwards' or 'towards'.

v. In To/Into

<u>In</u> <u>to</u> and <u>into</u> mean two different things.

<u>In</u> <u>to</u> - means 'in order to' (<u>in</u> - preposition combined with adverb <u>to</u>).

<u>Into</u> - means 'movement' or 'transformation' (preposition of place).

If the word that follows <u>to</u> is a verb like run, walk, annoy, avoid, then do not join <u>in</u> and <u>to</u>.

Examples of correct usage:

Bill charged <u>into</u> John's shed.

Margery stayed <u>in</u> <u>to</u> avoid meeting Bill.

John escorted Margery <u>into</u> the restaurant.

EDIT: #51
Search for <u>into</u> and <u>in</u> <u>to</u>.
Make sure they are used correctly.
Remember: <u>In</u> <u>to</u> - means 'in order to'. <u>Into</u> - means 'movement' or 'transformation'

vi. Homophones

Words that are pronounced the same, but have different meanings and spellings are called 'homophones'. We can spellcheck our finished novel and get a green light, but a spellcheck will not flag up words that are spelled correctly, but used incorrectly.

Tricky.

For a long time I thought 'draw' (to create pictures with a pen/pencil) meant 'drawer' (a place to keep my socks).

I was mortified when I realised my mistake. Another one of mine was 'lead' - (a heavy metal) instead of 'led' - past tense of lead (as in leader). Ack.

Embarrassing.

There are hundreds of these. I don't want to waste space with pages and pages of them, so I will list a few examples to give you an idea what to look out for:

> Allowed: permitted.
> Aloud: out loud.
>
> Allude: to refer indirectly.
> Elude: to avoid capture.
>
> Bare: naked.
> Bear: grizzly animal.

Boar: wild pig.
Bore: uninteresting/boring/to drill.

Elicit: to bring out or evoke.
Illicit: unlawful.

Ensure: to guarantee an event or condition.
Insure: to provide with insurance.

Gorilla: big ape.
Guerrilla: urban warrior.

Hangar: a shed or shelter.
Hanger: an object to hang up clothes.

Heroin: an illegal narcotic.
Heroine: a heroic female.

Hoard: to stockpile something.
Horde: a throng or swarm.

Knew: did know.
New: not old.

Know: have knowledge.
No: opposite of yes.

Principal: foremost/first.
Principle: a moralistic belief

Raise: to bring up; to elevate; to increase.
Raze: to tear down completely.

Retch: to vomit.
Wretch: a miserable person.

Sea: an ocean.
See: observe.

Tenet: a principle, belief, or doctrine.
Tenant: one who rents or leases.

There: referring to a place.
Their: possessive case of they.

Thrown: lobbed, chucked.
Throne: A seat for royalty.

You're: contraction of you are.
Your: belonging to you.

Now you are aware of this problem (if you weren't before), you can keep an eye out for them.

EDIT: #52

Search for the example homophones detailed in this section. Make sure you are using the correct word.
Remember: Create a list of your most common homophones. Apply this list to your new fiction.

SECTION EIGHT
Initial pronouns, conjunctions & 'ings'

Words to watch out for when starting sentences in modern fiction.

In this section:

i. Initial Conjunctions
And... But... So... Huh? 181

ii. Initial 'ings'
Don't leave me hanging, dude 183

i. Initial Conjunctions

Conjunctions are the most gregarious of all words as their principal function is to bring sentences together. The most common are: <u>and</u>, <u>but</u>, <u>or</u>, <u>because</u>, <u>since</u>, <u>when</u>. They also include: <u>for</u>, <u>nor</u>, <u>or</u>, <u>yet</u>, <u>so</u>.

What are initial conjunctions?
They are conjunctions used by us pesky writers to start sentences instead of joining sentences together.

Examples:

<u>But</u> that was not enough for John.

<u>And</u> Bill did take Margery's advice.

<u>Yet</u> Bill's nemesis knew better.

<u>Nor</u> did Margery come home the next night.

Why do writers do this?
You can start a sentence in whatever way you desire as long as it's well-written. It is a stylish way of introducing a follow-on thought or the development of a narrative.

That's a good thing, right?
Yes and no.

We can treat initial conjunctions like any grammatical construction - they shouldn't be overdone.

Example:

And Bill did take Margery's advice. And the next day, he went down the Gym. And he ate less. And in two months he had lost one-stone. And he looked good.

Overuse can sound childlike. Use initial conjunctions well and they will work for you; use them badly and your writing will suffer.

One last thing
Anyone saying this is bad or incorrect writing is old fashioned and out of touch. It is perfectly acceptable

EDIT: #53
Search for the initial conjunctions (using 'match-case'):
For, And, Nor, But, Or, Yet and So.
Check for overuse.
Remember: Starting too many sentences with conjunctions can lend your writing a childish feel.

ii. Initial 'ings'

An initial <u>ing</u> is a participle (a word ending in <u>ing</u>) used as a noun at the start of a sentence. It is also known as a 'gerund'.

Is it bad grammar to start a sentence with a word ending in <u>ing</u>? No...but you need to be careful.

Example:

Sailing requires skill and intelligence.

The above example is perfectly acceptable. But using an initial ing in some sentences may lessen the impact.

Example:

Fleeing John's garden, Bill fell and knocked himself out.

The above example is grammatically correct, but because the active subject and verb do not precede the qualifying phrase, it commands less attention.

Let's switch it around:

Bill fell and knocked himself out while fleeing John's garden.

The active subject and verb now precedes the qualifying

phrase, and the line has more impact.

Initial <u>ings</u> are acceptable, but if they can be re-written for more effect, do so.

Anything Else?
DO NOT OVERUSE THEM! Sorry for the capitals, but as this is the main advice for most of this guide, I was a little shocked that you needed to ask.

EDIT: #54
Search for words ending in <u>ing</u> at the start of your sentences. If they can be re-written for more impact - then do so. Make sure you do not overuse them.

SUMMARY
One last, final, ultimate, closing, finishing EDIT…

Your finished, polished novel should now be relatively free of the more common signifiers of bad writing outlined in the above fifty-four copy-edits.

Readers will evaluate your novel purely on the strength of your story and not on clumsy prose, overuse of exclamation marks, repetition, flabbiness, etc. They may not notice why your fiction is more engaging, but subconsciously they will be responding to the improved flow, to the more immediate prose and the leaner sentences.

Fifty-four copy-edits?

Yes, we have one final, concluding, finishing, ultimate, closing sub:

FINAL EDIT - EDIT: #55
Put your novel away for at least two weeks.
Two weeks?
Yes.
I'd leave it for six weeks to be on the safe side. When the time is up, give your novel one final read through. Look for typos and changes that didn't quite work…and fix.
Remember: You're now an author. Enjoy that feeling.

I sincerely wish you the best of success with your novel(s) and all future writing endeavours.

FULL GLOSSARY OF EDITS
A full list of Copy-edits included in this guide

To effectively edit your manuscript, you need to read the supporting documentation behind each of these individual edits.

EDIT 1 - redundant adjectives
EDIT 2 - large/big/little/small
EDIT 3 - young/old
EDIT 4 - hot/cold/warm
EDIT 5 - happy/sad
EDIT 6 - stupid/thick/wide
EDIT 7 - beautiful/wonderful/pretty
EDIT 8 - horrid/horrible/terrible/dark
EDIT 9 - words ending in 'ly'
EDIT 10 - only
EDIT 11 - that
EDIT 12 - was/were
EDIT 13 - there is, there are & it is
EDIT 14 - it
EDIT 15 - had
EDIT 16 - up/down
EDIT 17 - in/out
EDIT 18 - over/under/below/beneath
EDIT 19 - on/off
EDIT 20 - of
EDIT 21 - felt/feel/feeling
EDIT 22 - look/looked/looking
EDIT 23 - watch/notice/observe
EDIT 24 - see/saw
EDIT 25 - hear/heard

EDIT 26 - smell/taste
EDIT 27 - knew/know, claim/claimed, believe/believed
EDIT 28 - quotation marks
EDIT 29 - emphasised italics
EDIT 30 - titles of works
EDIT 31 - foreign words, letters & sounds
EDIT 32 - titles & family names
EDIT 33 - directions
EDIT 34 - numbers
EDIT 35 - dialogue
EDIT 36 - exclamations
EDIT 37 - ellipsis
EDIT 38 - single word modifiers
EDIT 39 - however and nevertheless, moreover &
        furthermore
EDIT 40 - got
EDIT 41 - even
EDIT 42 - so
EDIT 43 - a lot/alot
EDIT 44 - almost/seemed/began/started
EDIT 45 - as
EDIT 46 - circumlocutions
EDIT 47 - affect/effect
EDIT 48- who/whom
EDIT 49 - all right/alright
EDIT 50 - on to/onto
EDIT 51 - in to/into
EDIT 52 - homophones
EDIT 53 - initial conjunctions
EDIT 54 - initial 'ing'
EDIT 55 - the bottom drawer

A Note from *K.J.Heritage*

If you enjoyed reading *All About Copywriting* as much as I did writing it, can I ask you to please leave a review. It really makes a difference, and writers always value a good honest critique.

Suffice it so say, if you leave me a review on any of the e-book stores, or Goodreads or anywhere else, I'll be *well-chuffed*.

Kev

For information on further releases, <u>please join my newsletter</u> and get a FREE COPY of my short story anthology, <u>*The Lady In The Glass – 12 Tales Of Death & Dying*</u>

Or you can pop over to my personal Facebook group, Mostly Readers. Where we chat and post about reading… *mostly:* <u>https://www.facebook.com/groups/mostlyreaders/</u>

And, of course, there is also my Twitter account @ <u>MostlyWriting</u> – with (just) over 100K followers!

Also free on Amazon:
<u>Flesh Golem (The Scowl: Part One - An introduction to the IronScythe Sagas)</u>

<u>Quick-Kill & The Galactic Secret Service (Part One)</u>

Keep reading for my full list of books and links.

Links

Join my Mostly Readers Club!
Get an inside track on all future releases, access to early reading copies (ARCs), sneak previews, and more.
http://mostlywriting.co.uk/join

Twitter:
Over 100,000 followers and growing
@MostlyWriting

Email:
Want to get in touch? Well here's your chance
contact@mostlywriting.co.uk

Facebook Group: Mostly Readers
Fun chat and posts about reading… *mostly.*
https://www.facebook.com/groups/mostlyreaders

BookBub:
Not only can you check out the latest cool book deals, but you can also get an alert when I publish my next book
https://www.bookbub.com/authors/k-j-heritage

Goodreads:
Friend me here:
https://www.goodreads.com/kjheritage

Amazon:
Click the **+Follow** button under my mostly sexy photograph
http://smarturl.it/amznkev

Acknowledgements

Thanks for the red-pen, scribbling and 'telling me off in no uncertain terms' talents of my lovely editor:

Suzanne Buist

Also by K.J.Heritage

Mystery and Crime
Dying Is Easy

Science Fiction
Shattered Helix (Vatic Book 1)
Shattered Web (Vatic Book 2)
Blue Into The Rip
Quick-Kill & The Galactic Secret Service
The Lady In The Glass - 12 Tales Of Death & Dying

Sci-Fi Compilations
Once Upon A Time In Gravity City
Chronicle Worlds: Legacy Fleet
From The Indie Side

Fantasy
The Scowl

Non-Fiction
All About Copywriting: 55 Easy Edits To Improve Your Writing Forever

Read on for more details.

Shattered Helix (Vatic Book 1)
The Amazon #1 Bestseller
He's a crack empath detective on the run. But when the soulless 'Company' bring him back to solve a complex murder, can Vatic escape with his life?

A distinguished Company scientist has been murdered.

Vatic, an on-the-run half-alive empath with no memory of who or what he is, will die in six-hours if he can't find out why—or so the Company tells him—an 'added incentive to get the job done'.

Our hero soon discovers he is one of the *Skilled*, a genetically enhanced human—revered and despised in equal measure—a bloodhound with a terrifying past who'll stop at nothing in his pursuit of truth.

And 'the Skilled always get their guy'… *don't they?*

Read what other bestselling authors are saying about *Shattered Helix*

"Gritty, intense, and compelling, Vatic is something you don't run into often enough in Sci-Fi--a cerebral thrill ride you don't want to end." - **Michael Bunker, US TODAY Bestselling author of Pennsylvania**

"Prepare to lose sleep reading Vatic! Delicious Sci-Fiction!" - **Kate Danley, US TODAY bestseling Author.**

"K.J.Heritage's uncanny sense of pacing and story puts him at the forefront of today's speculative fiction writers." **- Samuel Peralta, Amazon bestselling author and creator of The Future Chronicles**

"Gritty, detailed and unrelenting. Vatic will take you on a wild ride." **- Peter Cawdron, International Bestselling author of Science Fiction**

Shattered Web (Vatic Book 2)

Trapped on an insane Company bioship with a dead crew, murderous survivors and heading for certain destruction...just another day at the office for Vatic.

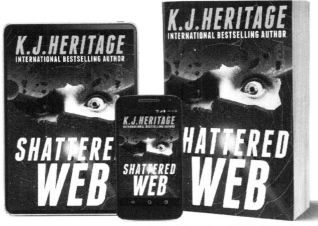

Experimental Company bioship, the *CSS Ariadne,* has cut all communications and launched herself into hyperspace--heading towards enemy territory and certain destruction if she cannot be stopped.

The crew managed to send out an SOS before the *Ariadne* disappeared. Someone was murdered... *but who?*

Vatic, a Skilled empath in the reluctant employ of the Company, is drugged and forced to board the rogue ship. He arrives to find the vessel full of corpses, a small band of suspicious survivors, and no explanations.

Our hero soon realises that not everyone who survived is as they seem. There is an imposter aboard, but who is it, and what are their motives?

Vatic must use all his talents if he and the ship are going to survive.

But survival is what the Skilled do best... isn't it?

Reviews

"Another fast paced, whirlwind of a story!"

"Very well written and extremely captivating! Fantastic 2nd book in the series."

"Mr. Heritage has done it again."

"Full of twists and turns like going down a rabbit hole"

"A plot that'll keep you on the edge of your seat"

"Boil the kettle, put your feet up, and take a voyage on the good ship Ariadne."

DYING IS EASY

He wanted to live happily-ever-after. Jozee wanted to leave. But when she mysteriously disappears, Adam finds himself in a desperate fight to save both their lives!

Up and coming comedy talent, Jozee Jackson's life seems almost perfect, until she disappears after a silly drunken argument with devoted boyfriend and new comedian, Adam Hanson.

Where has she gone? And why? Jozee loved their life together... *didn't she?*

Despite all his friends in the local stand-up scene believing Jozee had left him to pursue a new life, Adam suspects foul play and becomes determined to find his missing girlfriend.

After a series of shocking discoveries that shed a new and disturbing light on Jozee's private life, Adam begins to wonder if he knows his girlfriend at all.

Why are men from seedy hook-up websites visiting their flat when he's supposed to be at work? Who is behind the torrent of vile text messages and emails sent to Adam's phone? And what is the dark secret of Jozee's dead ex-boyfriend?

Adam won't give up looking until he finds answers to these questions - *no matter what the consequences.*

Reviews

"This is a truly unputdownable thriller."

"A wicked thriller with a sense of humour!"

"If you like your crime fiction gritty and uncompromising, then you'll like this one."

"The best time I've had sat on the train with a kindle."

"You'll never watch a stand-up performance again without wondering what nasty secrets lie beneath".

"An absolute gem and enjoyed it from start to finish"

"A surprise ending, but a satisfying one.

"A gripping mystery which gives an insight into the murky world of open mic stand-up comedy."

"The author clearly knows Brighton and stand up comedy well and draws up on both milieus with wit and authenticity"

"With a narrator who is a self confessed OCD sufferer and a panoply of 'suspects' for a crime that we're not even sure has actually taken place, we have the recipe for a gripping yarn that keeps us hanging on right up to the final page."

"This book was perfect. And with all the twists and turns throughout, I just didn't want to be put it down."

"A compelling read you're bound to enjoy. Download it now!"

"An excellent depiction of the open mike comedy circuit in Brighton as well as in London."

"I highly recommend this book, but keep your woobie close by, you're gonna need it!"

BLUE INTO THE RIP
Amazon #1 Bestseller

Blue is an angry, mixed up teen ripped 400 years from home. When the evil SEARCH corps try and use him to kill his parents, can he rescue them from certain death?

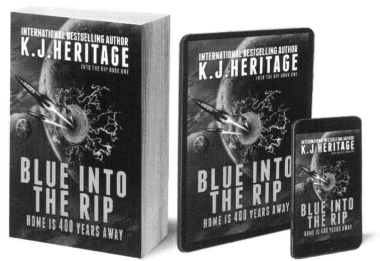

HOME IS 400 YEARS AWAY

A Rip in the fabric of time, a far-flung globally warmed future, a flooded Earth and the only remainder of civilisation—a militaristic organisation living underneath 'Desert Amazon'...

Getting back home was the only thing that mattered to messed up, mixed race teenager, Blue (named after his stupid, googly blue eyes) - and that was the problem—home was over four hundred years in the past.

But how does a lowly cadet in a military academy living

in a post-apocalyptic future achieve such a goal, especially with the distractions of girls, pilot training, spacewalks and his almost constant unpopularity?

The more Blue found out about this flooded, gung-ho and annoying future, about himself—who and what he was (was he even human?)—and the equally disturbing and shocking truth about his parents, the more he realised getting home was the only solution.

Wasn't it?

If Blue knew one thing, it was that he would at least try.

Reviews for Blue Into The Rip

"An amazing read and K.J.Heritage's writing is superb and unique...I definitely recommend this book to sci-fi adventure readers!" **Girl In The Woods**

"Hands-down one of the most creative YA books I've read in a long time." **Reading For Pleasure**

"Fast paced, intriguing, thought provoking, character driven science fiction. I loved it." **The Written Universe**

"A fun, addictive read from page one." **40 West Media**

"K.J.Heritage seems to understand that you don't need to go 'over the top' in order to make contact with the human heart." **The Underground Treehouse**

"It captivated me from the beginning and held me prisoner to the end!" Author Alliance

"This is one of those books and I was awake into the early hours reading. Young Adult time travel at its best." **A Woman's Wisdom**

"I was drawn in hook, line and sinker...an amazing story and a great ending." **Bookaholic Babe**

"A winner from the very beginning...an excellent piece of science-fiction that can be enjoyed by adults as well as teenagers." **My Writer's Cramp**

"The Rip? Awesome!" **Just Blogging**

"All the ingredients for a great sci-fi teen read...Highly enjoyable." **Liz Loves Books YA**

"Fun, heart-warming, made me want to turn the pages faster" **The Book Tart**

QUICK-KILL & THE
GALACTIC SECRET SERVICE
The Complete Four Book Series

Quick-Kill is a self-made assassin and tekhead. But after a simple job blows up in her face, she finds herself running for her life. A life that is changed forever.

And so begins a fun, fast-paced, action-stuffed, gender-bending futuristic four book thrill ride!

Never, ever, let yourself never get caught... who knows what may happen?

The forgotten, seedy backwater planet of Plenty (the most unfortunately-named world there ever was), is no place for a girl to grow up parentless and alone. But self-styled, femme fatale and genius gun-for hire, Quick-Kill Jane, was no normal kid. She learned her trade early on, making a name for herself. And by the time she became an adult, everyone feared and respected that name in equal measure.

In what should've been a straightforward job—one of the many she had built her reputation upon—she finds herself in pursuit of small-time criminal and wife-beater, Rollo Barla. But things do not go to plan.

She learns that the contract on Rollo was ordered by the Cabal—a loose network of galactic criminals, and that they, and the equally shady Galactic Secret Service, were now in competition to chase her down.

Quick-Kill must use all her considerable talents, skills and guile to stay one step ahead. But events take an unexpected and extraordinary turn.

A twist that will change Quick-Kill's life forever...

And so begins Quick-Kill's adventures.

Includes the books:
Quick-Kill
The "Do Or Die"
Bluetongue
Sirena

Reviews for Quick Kill & the Galactic Secret Service

"A well written rip-roaring tale with space ships, lasers, explosions and daring-do...what's not to like?"

"Fun, feisty and fast-moving, this is a highly enjoyable read"

"If you love fantasy or sci-fi, you have to read this book now!"

"A fast-paced, brilliant SciFi story"

"Bloody marvellous!"

The Scowl
IronScythe Sagas Books 1-3

If you like George R.R. Martin's *Game of Thrones,* R.E. Howard's *Conan the Barbarian,* or Michael Moorcock's *Stormbringer* - then this is a novel for you.

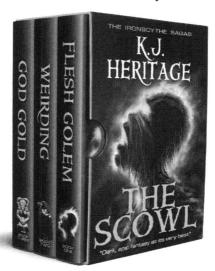

'And from the dark unknown came a hooded avenger, a sable-weaved nemesis branded with living iron whose will it was to destroy all works of delving. His name? He had many over his lifetime, but history only remembers him as— the Scowl.'

When the Scowl is brought before the court of King-Emperor Jhaz'Elrad, accused of murdering a young noble, he is unexpectedly saved from execution by the ambitious Dracus Krall.

In return for his life, the Scowl is sent on weregild to kill the evil golem that has lurked in the Krall family home for generations. A terrible, haunted creature, created by dark majiks in the time of Delving.

Accompanying the task is Dracus' teenage niece, Vareena, a strong-willed tom-boy who grew up in the shadow of her uncle's ambition and who has resisted his many attempts to marry her off.

But Vareena is not as she seems. She harbours a secret power that her uncle would gladly kill for.

Together, Vareena and the Scowl begin an uneasy alliance. An alliance that will change both of their lives forever...

Includes the books:
Flesh Golem
Weirding
God Gold

Reviews

"A fast-paced fantasy adventure that will thrill and delight readers from start to finish...The Scowl is a very exciting read for those who are into fantasy stories and a nice introduction to the genre for non-fans, too."
Reading For Pleasure

"If you love the genre of Adult Fantasy then you must give K.J.Heritage's books a go. Heritage really does bring dark fantasy to life."
A Woman's Wisdom

Other reader reviews
"K.J.Heritage has a wonderful ability to bring characters to life and the way he keeps the action moving at a pace is mind blowing!"

"A captivating plot, complex characters, and a creative world made it so I did not want to put this novel down. I was hooked right away..."

"One of the best new fantasy books I've read in a while."

"If you love the genre of Adult Fantasy then you must give K.J.Heritage's books a go. Heritage really does bring dark fantasy to life with descriptive prose which draws you in and keeps you there until the book is done."

"K.J.Heritage is an amazing story teller. He makes you care about the characters and want to learn more as the tale unfolds. I'm looking forward to reading future installments of the Ironsythe Sagas. I highly recommend this book."

"I love this series by K.J.Heritage! The world he creates for the reader is so vivid and quirky, and packed with amazing characters and exciting action. If you like fantasy, or even if you don't, this is the series for you!"

About K.J.Heritage

"K.J.Heritage's uncanny sense of pacing and story puts him at the forefront of today's speculative fiction writers."

Samuel Peralta, Amazon bestselling author and creator of The Future Chronicles

K.J.Heritage writes books that he loves to read. From science fiction action and adventure mysteries to contemporary thrillers and paranormal fantasy.

His first sci-fi short story, *Escaping The Cradle* was runner-up in the 2005 Clarke-Bradbury International Science Fiction Competition.

He has also appeared in several anthologies with such self-publishing sci-fi luminaries as Hugh Howey, Michael Bunker and Samuel Peralta.

He has done all the requisite 'writery' jobs such as driver's mate, factory gateman, barman, labourer, telesales operative, sales assistant, warehouseman, IT contractor, Student Union President, university IT helpdesk guy, British Rail signal software designer, premiership football website designer, gigging musician, graphic designer, stand-up comedian, sound engineer, improv artist, magazine editor and web journo... Although he doesn't like to talk about it. *Mostly*.

He was born in the UK in one of the more interesting

previous centuries. Originally from Derbyshire, he now lives in the seaside town of Brighton. He is a tea drinker, avid Twitterer, and autistic spectrum (ASD) human being.

FOR ALL media enquiries, event/booking information, signed copies, etc. please email: contact@mostlywriting.co.uk

All the very best,

K.J.Heritage

Printed in Great Britain
by Amazon

The
Speedy
Question
Bank

Key Stage 3
Tier 5–7

Speedy Revision

Introduction

This question bank is aimed at Tier 5–7 of the KS3 National Tests for Mathematics. It's the perfect size to keep with you at all times during the crucial weeks before the tests.

There is *speedy* coverage of each topic in the four main strands:
- Number
- Algebra
- Shape, space & measures
- Handling data

Speed-up sheets

The idea behind this book is simple: to provide the *speediest* practice possible. To this end, some questions have a mouse symbol, 🐭, next to them. This indicates that a *speed*-up sheet is available for download from our website.

Go to
www.brookworth.co.uk/speedup.html
for links to all the *speed*-up sheets.

The *speed*-up sheets provide blank axes, diagrams to complete and so on. And of course they are all free!

Answers to all questions can be found at the back of the book, so that you can check that you're on the right track.

Good luck in your tests!

Contents

Number
Special numbers 4
Multiples, factors &
  prime factors 4
LCM & HCF 5
Multiplying & dividing by
  10, 100, 1000, ... 5
Rounding 6
Fractions 7
Percentages 9
Fractions, decimals &
  percentages 10
Ratio & proportion 11
Negative numbers 12
Powers & roots 13
Standard index form 13
Written methods 14
Calculations with brackets 15

Algebra
Using letters 16
Brackets 17
Equations 17
Formulae & substitution 18
Rearranging formulae 19
Sequences &
  number patterns 20
Functions & mappings 21
Coordinates 22
Straight-line graphs 23
Real-life graphs 25
Inequalities 26
Trial & improvement 26

Shape, space & measures
Units of measurement 27
Reading scales & accuracy 28

Estimating &
  measuring angles 29
Angles & parallel lines 29
Polygons 31
Symmetry & properties of
  shapes 32
Reflection 34
Rotation 35
Translation 36
Enlargement 37
Perimeter & circumference 38
Areas of triangles &
  quadrilaterals 39
Areas of circles &
  composite shapes 40
More circles 40
Pythagoras' theorem 41
Nets & 3-D shapes; plans &
  elevations 42
Volume & surface area 43
Bearings & scale drawings 45
Compound measures 46
Constructions & loci 46

Handling data
Mean, median, mode, range 48
Collecting data &
  two-way tables 49
Frequency tables 50
Bar charts & frequency
  diagrams 51
Stem & leaf diagrams; line
  graphs 52
Pie charts 53
Scatter graphs 54
Probability 55

Answers 56

Special numbers

1 Name the sequence and fill in the missing numbers:
  a 1, 4, 9, ..., 25, ..., ..., 64, ..., 100
  b 1, 3, 6, 10, ..., ..., 28, 36, ..., ...

2 List the prime numbers up to 30.

3 10, 43, 17, 25, 23, 64, 36
  From the list, write down the
  a prime numbers   **b** square numbers   **c** triangular numbers.

Multiples, factors & prime factors

1 List the first five multiples of these:
a	9	**b**	4	**c**	10	**d**	7
e	6	**f**	11	**g**	3	**h**	20

2 Write true or false for each of these:
  a 2 is a factor of 318.   **b** 10 is a factor of 50.
  c 3 is a factor of 46.   **d** 2 is a factor of 199.
  e 5 is a factor of 1000.   **f** 4 is a factor of 82.
  g 5 is a factor of 51.   **h** 9 is a factor of 126.

3 List all the factors of these:
a	27	**b**	14	**c**	36	**d**	20
e	100	**f**	63	**g**	49	**h**	44

4 A prime number has exactly two factors.
  List the factors of these and state whether they are prime:
  a 47   **b** 51   **c** 39   **d** 37

5 3, 18, 25, 27, 32, 12
  From the list of numbers, find any
  a factors of 36   **b** multiples of 4.

6 Write these as products of their prime factors:
a	28	**b**	105	**c**	54	**d**	78
e	100	**f**	46	**g**	140	**h**	90

7 $5^3 \times 7$ is the prime factorisation of 875.
  What number is 2×7^3 the prime factorisation of?

LCM & HCF

1 What is the Least Common Multiple (LCM) of
    a 3 and 9   **b** 5 and 8
    c 8 and 12   **d** 16 and 24
    e 15 and 35   **f** 14 and 21
    g 40 and 100   **h** 25 and 30?

2 What is the Highest Common Factor (HCF) of
    a 12 and 18   **b** 25 and 35
    c 36 and 60   **d** 21 and 49
    e 32 and 48   **f** 13 and 63
    g 42 and 70   **h** 60 and 105?

3 A bell rings every 15 minutes.
Another bell rings every 25 minutes.
If both bells ring at 09:00, when will they next ring at the same time?

Multiplying & dividing by 10, 100, 1000, ...

1 Multiply:
    a 54 × 10   **b** 9 × 1000   **c** 5 × 100
    d 6.3 × 10   **e** 0.8 × 100   **f** 0.2 × 1000
    g 0.32 × 100   **h** 0.045 × 1000   **i** 5.06 × 10

2 Divide:
    a 400 ÷ 100   **b** 96 ÷ 10   **c** 20 000 ÷ 1000
    d 319 ÷ 10   **e** 24.8 ÷ 10   **f** 71 ÷ 100
    g 111 ÷ 100   **h** 4160 ÷ 100   **i** 5100 ÷ 1000

3 Multiply:
    a 9 × 600   **b** 11 × 70   **c** 3 × 8000
    d 7 × 3000   **e** 5 × 400   **f** 18 × 0.1
    g 106.9 × 0.1   **h** 27 × 0.01   **i** 2.6 × 0.01

4 Divide:
    a 1600 ÷ 40   **b** 360 ÷ 900   **c** 33 000 ÷ 3000
    d 24 ÷ 80   **e** 48 000 ÷ 600   **f** 380 ÷ 2000
    g 10.8 ÷ 0.1   **h** 2.19 ÷ 0.01   **i** 0.57 ÷ 0.1

Rounding

1 Round these to the nearest 10:
   a 32   **b** 65   **c** 1071   **d** 239
   e 4015   **f** 51.69   **g** 28 562   **h** 7.9068

2 Round these to the nearest 100:
   a 472   **b** 801   **c** 95.14   **d** 17.2
   e 1250   **f** 5001   **g** 20 687   **h** 322.99

3 Round these to the nearest 1000:
   a 2069   **b** 5009   **c** 1400   **d** 499.8
   e 12 004   **f** 7386   **g** 6915   **h** 31 239

4 Round these to the nearest whole number:
   a 0.9   **b** 2.63   **c** 10.5   **d** 1.08
   e 7.614   **f** 0.9527   **g** 12.103   **h** 16.591

5 Round these to 1 d.p.
   a 6.18   **b** 0.594   **c** 1.42   **d** 2.653
   e 3.84   **f** 24.79   **g** 7.0516   **h** 301.63

6 Round these to 2 d.p.
   a 1.438   **b** 9.026   **c** 4.9415   **d** 10.835
   e 0.6104   **f** 2.9945   **g** 12.095   **h** 1.7216

7 Round these to 1 s.f.
   a 25 172   **b** 10.965   **c** 0.1093   **d** 2499

8 Round these to 2 s.f.
   a 0.9865   **b** 2.0631   **c** 214.17   **d** 27 669

9 Round these to 3 s.f.
   a 1236   **b** 0.705 41 **c** 33 333.3 **d** 9.607 29

10 The diameter of a circle is 4.8 cm.
The calculation to find the
circumference is 3.142 × 4.8.
Estimate the circumference by
rounding to 1 s.f.

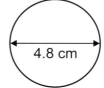

4.8 cm

11 The calculation to find the area of the circle in question **10** is
3.142 × 2.4^2.
Estimate the area by rounding to 1 s.f.

Fractions

1 Write two equivalent fractions for the shaded part:

a   **b**   **c**

d   **e**   **f**

2 Copy these and finish simplifying the fractions:

a
$$\overset{\div 3}{\frac{3}{6}} = \frac{\square}{2}$$
$$\underset{\div 3}{}$$

b
$$\overset{\div 4}{\frac{4}{8}} = \frac{1}{\square}$$
$$\underset{\div 4}{}$$

c
$$\overset{\div 4}{\frac{8}{20}} = \frac{\square}{\square}$$
$$\underset{\div 4}{}$$

d
$$\overset{\div 2}{\frac{2}{14}} = \frac{\square}{\square}$$
$$\underset{\div 2}{}$$

e
$$\overset{\div \square}{\frac{5}{20}} = \frac{1}{4}$$
$$\underset{\div \square}{}$$

f
$$\overset{\div \square}{\frac{8}{12}} = \frac{\square}{3}$$
$$\underset{\div \square}{}$$

3 Write as a fraction in its simplest form:

a $\frac{6}{8}$ **b** $\frac{2}{12}$ **c** $\frac{10}{30}$

d $\frac{3}{18}$ **e** $\frac{9}{27}$ **f** $\frac{6}{24}$

g 6p out of 10p **h** 5p out of 50p **i** 25p out of £1

4 Write these mixed numbers as improper fractions:

a $1\frac{1}{2}$ **b** $1\frac{1}{3}$ **c** $1\frac{3}{4}$

d $1\frac{2}{5}$ **e** $2\frac{1}{6}$ **f** $2\frac{3}{7}$

g $2\frac{5}{8}$ **h** $3\frac{1}{10}$ **i** $3\frac{2}{9}$

5 Write these improper fractions as mixed numbers:

a $\frac{11}{3}$ **b** $\frac{13}{2}$ **c** $\frac{25}{6}$

d $\frac{17}{5}$ **e** $\frac{20}{9}$ **f** $\frac{21}{4}$

g $\frac{10}{4}$ **h** $\frac{19}{8}$ **i** $\frac{22}{7}$

continued ➤

Fractions (continued)

6 Add these then give the answer in its simplest form:

    a $\frac{1}{4} + \frac{1}{8}$ **b** $\frac{2}{3} + \frac{1}{6}$ **c** $\frac{2}{5} + \frac{1}{10}$

    d $\frac{2}{3} + \frac{5}{6}$ **e** $\frac{1}{2} + \frac{1}{4} + \frac{1}{8}$ **f** $\frac{1}{2} + \frac{1}{5} + \frac{1}{10}$

    g $\frac{1}{2} + \frac{1}{3}$ **h** $\frac{2}{7} + \frac{1}{5}$ **i** $\frac{3}{4} + \frac{2}{3}$

7 Give each answer in its simplest form:

    a $\frac{2}{3} - \frac{5}{9}$ **b** $\frac{4}{6} - \frac{1}{2}$ **c** $\frac{7}{10} - \frac{2}{5}$

    d $\frac{6}{12} - \frac{1}{3}$ **e** $\frac{9}{10} - \frac{1}{2}$ **f** $1\frac{1}{8} - \frac{1}{4}$

    g $\frac{1}{2} + \frac{1}{4} - \frac{1}{8}$ **h** $\frac{1}{3} + \frac{1}{6} - \frac{1}{12}$ **i** $\frac{4}{5} - \frac{3}{4}$

8 Put these in order, smallest first:

    a $\frac{1}{2}$ $\frac{9}{12}$ $\frac{2}{3}$

    b $\frac{11}{18}$ $\frac{4}{9}$ $\frac{2}{3}$

    c $\frac{3}{4}$ $\frac{13}{20}$ $\frac{3}{5}$

9 Find: **a** $\frac{1}{3}$ of £90   **b** $\frac{2}{3}$ of £90

10 Find: **a** $\frac{1}{4}$ of 100 m   **b** $\frac{3}{4}$ of 100 m

11 Find: **a** $\frac{1}{5}$ of 35 mm   **b** $\frac{2}{5}$ of 35 mm

12 Find: **a** $\frac{1}{10}$ of 40p   **b** $\frac{7}{10}$ of 40p

13 What is $\frac{2}{3}$ of 360°?

14 What is $\frac{3}{5}$ of 50 g?

15 Give the answers to these multiplications in simplest form:

    a $\frac{1}{2} \times \frac{1}{3}$ **b** $\frac{1}{3} \times \frac{2}{5}$ **c** $\frac{2}{3} \times \frac{3}{7}$

    d $\frac{3}{4} \times \frac{1}{3}$ **e** $\frac{1}{6} \times \frac{3}{5}$ **f** $\frac{2}{5} \times \frac{5}{9}$

16 Do these divisions:

    a $\frac{1}{3} \div \frac{1}{2}$ **b** $\frac{1}{2} \div \frac{5}{7}$ **c** $\frac{1}{5} \div \frac{3}{4}$

    d $\frac{2}{3} \div \frac{5}{7}$ **e** $2\frac{1}{2} \div \frac{1}{4}$ **f** $2\frac{1}{2} \div \frac{3}{4}$

Percentages

1 In a class of 30 students, 12 are girls.
What percentage of the class are girls?

2 In a pack of 52 playing cards, 13 are Spades.
What percentage of the pack are Spades?

3 A sofa is priced at £2499.
In a sale, the price of the sofa is reduced by £749.
What percentage is this to the nearest whole number?

4 Find:
  a 27% of 800 ml   **b** 30% of £485
  c 4% of 150 g   **d** 72% of 25 mm
  e 21% of £450   **f** 5.9% of 30 m

5 What is 17.5% of £25?
Give your answer to the nearest penny.

6 Increase:
  a 30p by 10%   **b** 15 mm by 20%
  c 120 g by 5%   **d** 80 m by 2.5%
  e £48 by 30%   **f** 50 litres by 17%

7 Decrease:
  a 70p by 10%   **b** 60 mm by 5%
  c £24 by 2%   **d** 140 g by 15%
  e £20 000 by 8%   **f** 50 litres by 0.1%

8 In a sale, all prices are reduced by 20%.
What is the sale price of a T-shirt that originally cost £12?

9 A plant was 84 mm tall in April.
By May, the plant was 25% taller.
How tall was the plant in May?

10 A bank account pays 5% interest.
There is £230 in the account before interest is added.
How much is in the account after interest is added?

11 A fax machine costs £89 plus VAT.
If VAT is charged at 17.5%, how much does the fax machine
cost? Give your answer to the nearest penny.

Fractions, decimals & percentages

1 Convert these fractions to decimals:

a $\frac{1}{100}$ b $\frac{1}{8}$ c $\frac{3}{5}$ d $\frac{7}{8}$

e $\frac{3}{20}$ f $\frac{27}{50}$ g $\frac{1}{3}$ h $\frac{3}{10}$

2 Convert these percentages to fractions in their simplest form:

a 17%   b 23%   c 3%   d 129%

e 30%   f 75%   g 15%   h 112%

3 Convert these fractions to percentages:

a $\frac{5}{100}$ b $\frac{62}{100}$ c $\frac{118}{100}$ d $2\frac{94}{100}$

e $\frac{3}{10}$ f $\frac{1}{3}$ g $\frac{4}{5}$ h $\frac{3}{2}$

4 Convert these percentages to decimals:

a 40%   b 25%   c 90%   d 60%

e 5%   f 18%   g 3.2%   h 199%

5 Convert these decimals to fractions:

a 0.5   b 0.1   c 0.75   d 0.7

e 0.6   f 0.13   g 0.49   h 0.45

6 Which is the bigger amount: 25% of £60 or $\frac{2}{5}$ of £40?

7 Write these in order, smallest first:

a 0.5, 80%, 27%, $\frac{2}{3}$

b $4\frac{1}{2}$, 39.9%, 0.51, $\frac{41}{10}$

c 0.75, 8.6%, $\frac{20}{3}$, 18%

8 Which calculation can be used to find 18% of 40?

a 40 × 1.8   b 40 × 0.18   c 40 × 0.018

9 Increasing 30 by 5% is the same as finding 105%.
Which calculation can be used to increase 30 by 5%?

a 30 × 0.05   b 30 × 1.5   c 30 × 1.05

10 Decreasing 200 by 17% is the same as finding 83%.
Which calculation can be used to decrease 200 by 17%?

a 200 × 0.83   b 200 × 1.83   c 200 × 1.17

Ratio & proportion

1 a What proportion of the squares in this pattern are grey?
Give your answer as a fraction in its simplest form.

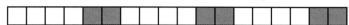

b What proportion of the squares are white?
Give your answer as a percentage to the nearest whole number.

c What is the ratio of grey squares to white squares?
Give your answer in its simplest form.

2 In a class there are 16 boys and 14 girls.
Write the ratio of boys to girls in its simplest form.

3 On a bus, there are 20 people. 12 are female.
Write the ratio of females to males in its simplest form.

4 The angles of a triangle are 30°, 60° and 90°.
Write the ratio of the angles in its simplest form.

5 Simplify these ratios:

a 16 : 40	**b** 12 : 15 : 75	**c** 63 cm : 14 cm
d 80p : £1.20	**e** 2 kg : 650 g	**f** 350 ml : 0.5 litre
g 2.1 cm : 1.8 cm	**h** €3.50 : €5.00	**i** 25 mm : 0.1 m

6 Dom and Sarah share a 360 ml drink in the ratio 4 : 5.
How much of the drink did Dom have?

7 In a triangle, the ratio of the angles is 7 : 9 : 20.
Calculate the angles.

8 An alloy is made from iron, copper and aluminium in the ratio
8 : 5 : 3. What percentage of the alloy is copper?

9 4 kg of red onions cost £1.40.
How much would 3 kg of red onions cost?

10 0.5 kg of apples costs 60p.
How much would 5 kg cost?

11 5 chocolate bars cost £1.60.
How much would 9 chocolate bars cost?

Ratio & proportion (continued)

12 A recipe for 4 people uses 160 g of soya mince.
How much soya mince is needed for 7 people?

13 Sanjiv is 120 cm tall and Isaac is 125 cm tall.
  a Write the ratio of Sanjiv's height to Isaac's height in its
  simplest form.

Ten years later, Sanjiv is $\frac{3}{8}$ taller and Isaac is 40% taller.
  b Find the new height ratio.
  Give your answer in its simplest form.

14 Write the ratio
area of parallelogram : area of triangle
in its simplest form.

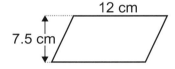
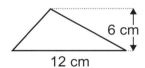

Negative numbers

1 **a** Write this list of numbers in order of size, smallest first:

  −1, 4, −3, 1, 2

  b What is the total of the numbers in part **a**?

2 The temperature is −3°C. It rises by 10°C. What is the new
temperature?

3 Work out the following:
  a 4 − 10   **b** −10 + 20   **c** −12 + 20
  d −10 − 20   **e** −9 − 12   **f** 4 − 5 − 8
  g −3 + 8 − 7   **h** 4 + −1   **i** −8 + −7
  j 1 + −5 + 3   **k** −6 − −3   **l** 7 − −9

4 **a** What number is halfway between −4 and 12?
  b 3 is halfway between two numbers.
  If one of the numbers is −7, what is the other number?

Speedy Revision

Powers & roots

1 Find these powers without using a calculator:
 a 7^2 **b** 5^3 **c** 10^3 **d** 24^0
 e 2^4 **f** 9^3 **g** 1^5 **h** 5^{-1}

2 Use the x^2 and x^y buttons on your calculator for these:
 a 23^2 **b** 8^3 **c** 5^4 **d** 0.5^{-2}
 e 11^3 **f** 4^5 **g** 0.5^4 **h** 1.1^3

3 Find these roots without using a calculator:
 a $\sqrt{16}$ **b** $25^{\frac{1}{2}}$ **c** $\sqrt[3]{64}$ **d** $1000^{\frac{1}{3}}$

4 Use the $\sqrt{}$ button on your calculator to find these:
 a $\sqrt{225}$ **b** $\sqrt{400}$ **c** $\sqrt{1681}$ **d** $\sqrt{0.09}$

5 Find these square roots to the accuracy given in brackets:
 a $\sqrt{145}$ (to 2 d.p.)   **b** $\sqrt{0.7}$ (to 2 s.f.)
 c $\sqrt{5}$ (to 1 s.f.)   **d** $\sqrt{117}$ (to 3 s.f.)

6 Combine these powers:
 a $3^4 \times 3^2$ **b** $4^5 \div 4^3$ **c** $2^8 \times 2^3$ **d** $(3^2)^4$
 e $7^6 \div 7^2$ **f** $(12^5)^3$ **g** $9^0 \times 9^5$ **h** $15^7 \div 15^4$

Standard index form

1 Write these as powers of 10:
 a 100   **b** 0.1   **c** 0.01   **d** 10 000

2 Write down the value of these:
 a 6×10^2 **b** 4×10^3 **c** 2.6×10^4
 d 3.8×10^5 **e** 6.7×10^{-1} **f** 8.3×10^{-2}

3 Finish writing these numbers in standard index form:
 a $210 = ? \times 10^2$ **b** $3800 = ? \times 10^3$
 c $450 = 4.5 \times 10^?$ **d** $0.6 = ? \times 10^{-1}$
 e $0.09 = 9 \times 10^?$ **f** $170 = ? \times 10^?$

4 A bag of potatoes weighs 4800 g. Write this in standard form.

5 A light year is 9.46×10^{12} km. Write this as a normal number.

6 Which is bigger:
 a 1.9×10^{-1} or 0.21   **b** 2.7×10^3 or 1.8×10^4?

Written methods

1 Use a written method to add these:
    a 1.36 + 1.42   **b** 21.7 + 18.2
    c 5.93 + 2.04   **d** 8.37 + 2.15
    e 5.91 + 3.24   **f** 6.81 + 2.36
    g 3.09 + 2.18   **h** 54.7 + 13.5

2 Use a written method to subtract these:
    a 4.96 − 3.12   **b** 6.19 − 2.08
    c 7.83 − 5.71   **d** 7.94 − 3.75
    e 12.71 − 5.09   **f** 36.9 − 17.46
    g 20.4 − 13.21   **h** 259.08 − 28.16

3 Use a written method to multiply these:
    a 39 × 7   **b** 42 × 9   **c** 26 × 17   **d** 34 × 21
    e 28 × 24 **f** 316 × 8 **g** 120 × 19 **h** 241 × 16

4 Use a written method to multiply these:
    a 2.6 × 7 **b** 4.1 × 6 **c** 3.7 × 8   **d** 4.9 × 5
    e 3.06 × 9 **f** 1.29 × 8 **g** 2.31 × 7 **h** 4.12 × 6

5 Use a written method to work out:
    a 126 ÷ 3 **b** 133 ÷ 7 **c** 162 ÷ 6 **d** 153 ÷ 9
    e 245 ÷ 5 **f** 104 ÷ 4 **g** 128 ÷ 7 **h** 71 ÷ 3
    i 139 ÷ 8 **j** 206 ÷ 5 **k** 124 ÷ 6 **l** 125 ÷ 4

6 Use a written method to work out:
    a 7.2 ÷ 4   **b** 22.5 ÷ 9 **c** 91.7 ÷ 7 **d** 69.6 ÷ 6
    e 175.2 ÷ 8 **f** 151.2 ÷ 9 **g** 16.5 ÷ 0.3 **h** 24.48 ÷ 1.2

7 David is saving up to buy an MP3 player which costs
£182.60. He has saved £76.18 so far.
How much more does he need to save?

8 Colleen is planning a picnic.
A bottle of lemonade costs £2.35.
Find how much 7 bottles of lemonade will cost.

9 The bill at a restaurant is £99.40.
7 people pay an equal share of the bill.
How much does each person pay?

Calculations with brackets

1 Calculate these mentally, using a written method or on a calculator. Give your answers to 2 d.p. where necessary.

a $18 + 4 \div 2$ **b** $5 \times (2 + 6)$

c $16 - (3 + 9)$ **d** $3 \times (4 + 2) - 7$

e $(15 + 7)(11 - 2)$ **f** $(14 - 6)^2$

g $4.9 \times (6.5^2 + 1.2)$ **h** $-4 \div (1.5 + 6)$

i $\sqrt{3^2 + 4^2}$ **j** $\sqrt{7.9^2 - 2.8^2}$

2 Insert brackets if they are needed:

a $8 \times 4 + 6 = 80$ **b** $3 + 8 \times 12 = 132$

c $36 \div 6 + 3 = 4$ **d** $4 \times 5 - 18 \div 3 = 14$

e $7 \times 8 - 3 \div 5 = 7$ **f** $30 - 20 \div 2^2 = 25$

g $8 + 7 - 3 \times 4 = 48$ **h** $-3 + 5 \times 8 + 4 = 24$

3 Estimate the answer to each of these:

a $\dfrac{5.29 + 8.62}{10.16 - 7.94}$ **b** $\dfrac{2.4 + 3.6^2}{2.8 \times 3.1}$

c $\dfrac{5^2 - 0.8}{13.8 - 6.1}$ **d** $\dfrac{17.2 + 14.9}{(3.7 - 1.8)^2}$

4 Use your calculator to find the answers to question **3** to 3 s.f.

5 Kelly wants to use these formulae:

$$A = \tfrac{1}{2}ab + \frac{\pi b^2}{8} \qquad\qquad P = a + \tfrac{1}{2}\pi b + \sqrt{a^2 + b^2}$$

to find the area (A) and perimeter (P) of shapes like this:

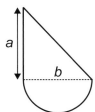

Kelly's first shape has $a = 4.5$, $b = 3$.

a Use the formula to work out the area of this shape:

$$A = \tfrac{1}{2} \times 4.5 \times 3 + \frac{3.14 \times 3^2}{8}$$

b Use the formula to work out the perimeter of this shape:

$$P = 4.5 + \tfrac{1}{2} \times 3.14 \times 3 + \sqrt{4.5^2 + 3^2}$$

Using letters

1 Simplify these expressions by collecting like terms:

a $10s + 1 - 2s + 5$ **b** $8 + a + 4a - 2$

c $2n + 1 + 2n + 1$ **d** $m + 5m + m + 3 - 1$

e $7 + b + 8b - 2b - 5$ **f** $3c + 3 + c + 3c$

g $6t + 2t + 3 - t + 4 + t$ **h** $g + g + 8 + 3g - g$

i $4n + 6 - 2n + 3$ **j** $5 - 3y - 8 + y$

2 Write expressions for the perimeters of these shapes:

a

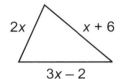

b

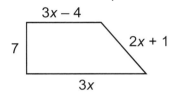

c

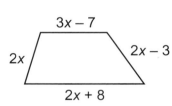

d

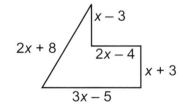

3 Find the length of the missing side:

a

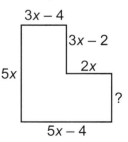

b

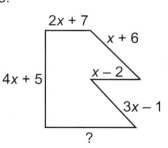

4 Add these fractions:

a $\frac{x}{5} + \frac{x}{5}$ **b** $\frac{x}{3} + \frac{x}{3}$ **c** $\frac{2x}{8} + \frac{x}{8}$

d $\frac{z}{7} + \frac{z}{7} + \frac{z}{7}$ **e** $\frac{4d}{10} + \frac{3d}{10}$ **f** $\frac{5n}{2} + \frac{4n}{2}$

g $\frac{8a}{3} - \frac{a}{3}$ **h** $\frac{3a}{4} + \frac{2a}{4}$ **i** $\frac{4m}{9} - \frac{3m}{9}$

Brackets

1 Multiply out these brackets:
- **a** $2(x + 1)$
- **b** $5(y - 3)$
- **c** $3(n + 2)$
- **d** $8(a - b)$
- **e** $-4(c + 1)$
- **f** $6(x + 5)$
- **g** $-3(z + 4)$
- **h** $10(w - 1)$
- **i** $-2(t - 1)$

2 Simplify these expressions:
- **a** $3(a + 1) + 2$
- **b** $2(n - 3) + n$
- **c** $5(4 - p) - 8$
- **d** $10 - 2(z + 1)$
- **e** $4(y + 3) - 3(y + 2)$
- **f** $5(s - 2) + 3(s - 1)$
- **g** $b(b - 6) + 2b$
- **h** $2a(b + 1) - 3a$

3 Multiply out these brackets and simplify:
- **a** $(x + 1)(x + 3)$
- **b** $(x + 5)(x + 2)$
- **c** $(x + 4)(x - 2)$
- **d** $(x + 1)(x - 1)$
- **e** $(x + 2)(x + 2)$
- **f** $(x + 5)^2$

Equations

1 Solve these equations:
- **a** $x + 8 = 10$
- **b** $5x = 50$
- **c** $3p = 9$
- **d** $m + 5 = 9$
- **e** $p - 2 = 31$
- **f** $2x = 18$
- **g** $3y = 27$
- **h** $c - 4 = 3$
- **i** $4y = 16$
- **j** $a + 14 = 30$

2 Solve these equations:
- **a** $2x + 1 = 5$
- **b** $5x - 1 = 19$
- **c** $3x - 3 = 9$
- **d** $4x + 5 = 25$
- **e** $2x + 8 = 28$
- **f** $7x - 2 = 12$
- **g** $3x + 7 = 34$
- **h** $8x - 4 = 36$
- **i** $5x - 7 = 33$
- **j** $9x + 2 = 29$

3 Solve these equations:
- **a** $2x = x + 3$
- **b** $3x = 2x + 7$
- **c** $5x = 4x + 11$
- **d** $6x = x + 10$
- **e** $13x = x + 48$
- **f** $4x = x + 15$
- **g** $7x = 4x + 12$
- **h** $12x = 7x + 25$
- **i** $9x = 2x + 14$
- **j** $10x = 3x + 42$

continued ➤➤➤

Equations (continued)

4 Solve these equations:

a $2(x + 1) = 6$ b $5(x - 2) = 35$

c $3(x + 5) = 27$ d $6(x + 4) = 42$

e $4(x - 8) = 12$ f $7(x - 3) = 14$

g $3(2x + 1) = 3$ h $10(9x + 1) = 100$

i $2(3x - 9) = 6$ j $4(2x + 1) = 20$

5 Here is a regular hexagon:

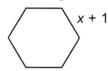

$x + 1$

The length of each side of the hexagon is $(x + 1)$ metres.

a Write an expression for the perimeter of the hexagon in terms of x.

b Find the value of x if the perimeter of the hexagon is 42 m.

Formulae & substitution

1 Substitute $m = 8$ into each of these expressions:

a $2m + 3$ b $7m - 5$ c $4m + 6$

d $3m + 5$ e $10m - 12$ f $9m - 6$

g $2m + 14$ h $3m - 5$ i $5m + 9$

2 Use the formula

$k = 1.6m$ where k = number of kilometres, m = number of miles

to convert these lengths to kilometres:

a 20 miles   b 5 miles   c 1.5 miles

d 10 miles   e 0.8 mile   f 2.25 miles

3 A joiner charges £22 per hour.

a Write a formula for the charge, C, in terms of the number of hours worked, h.

b Use your formula to work out the charge for 5 hours.

c Use your formula to work out the charge for 7 hours.

continued ➤➤➤

Formulae & substitution (continued)

4 This is the formula for finding speed:

Speed = Distance ÷ Time

a A car travels 180 miles in 3 hours.
What is the speed of the car?

b Re-write this formula using the letters S = Speed,
D = Distance, T = Time.

c Find S if D = 100 miles, T = 4 hours.

d Find S if D = 89 metres, T = 10 seconds.

5 Substitute $p = 2$, $q = 3$, $r = 5$ into these expressions:

a p^2 **b** $2q^2$ **c** $2 + r^2$

d $10(p + q)$ **e** $r^2 - p$ **f** $8pq$

6 This is the formula for finding the volume of a cube:

$V = w^3$

Find the volume of a cube with w = 5 cm.

7 This formula can be used to change temperatures
from degrees Fahrenheit to degrees Celsius:

$C = \frac{5}{9}(F - 32)$

Use the formula to change 75°F to degrees Celsius.
Give your answer to the nearest whole number.

Rearranging formulae

1 The fomula for the perimeter of a triangle is $P = a + b + c$.
Rearrange the formula to make a the subject.

2 The formula for the circumference of a circle is $C = \pi d$.
Rearrange the formula to make d the subject.

3 The formula for the area of a circle is $A = \pi r^2$.
Rearrange the formula to make r the subject.

4 Make w the subject of $V = w^3$.

5 Make a the subject of each of these formulae:

a $3b + a = 5$ **b** $6 = b + 2a$ **c** $b = \sqrt{a}$

d $2ab = 4b^2$ **e** $b = (a + 1)^2$ **f** $100b^2 = 4a^2$

Sequences & number patterns

1 Write the next three terms for these linear sequences:

   a 4, 7, 10, 13, ...   **b** 9, 19, 29, 39, ...

   c 90, 85, 80, 75, ...   **d** 7, 12, 17, 22, ...

   e 20, 18, 16, 14, ...   **f** 14, 17, 20, 23, ...

2 Here is a sequence of diagrams:

   a Describe in words how the sequence grows.

   b Write an expression for the nth term of the pattern.

3 Here is a sequence of matchstick patterns:

   a Describe in words how the sequence grows.

   b Write an expression for the nth term of the pattern.

4 Write the first five terms of the sequence with nth term:

   a $10n$ **b** $2n + 1$ **c** $4n - 1$

   d $3n + 4$ **e** $20 - n$ **f** $5n - 2$

5 The nth term of a sequence is $100 - 2n$.

   Find these terms in the sequence:

   a 1st term   **b** 15th term   **c** 30th term

6 Work out the nth term in these linear sequences:

   a 2, 4, 6, 8, 10, ...   **b** 5, 10, 15, 20, 25, ...

   c 8, 9, 10, 11, 12, ...   **d** 101, 102, 103, 104, 105, ...

   e 3, 5, 7, 9, 11, ...   **f** 1, 3, 5, 7, 9, ...

7 Write the next three terms of these quadratic sequences:

   a 10, 40, 90, 160, ...   **b** 0, 3, 8, 15, ...

   c 3, 6, 11, 18, ...   **d** 5, 8, 13, 20, ...

8 Write the first five terms of the sequence with nth term:

   a $n^2 + 5$ **b** $3n^2$ **c** $n^2 - 2$

9 Find the nth terms of the sequences in question **7**.

Functions & mappings

1 Find the outputs for these function machines:

a

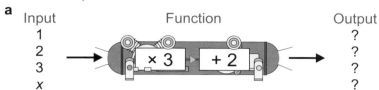

Input	Function	Output
1		?
2	×3 +2	?
3		?
x		?

b

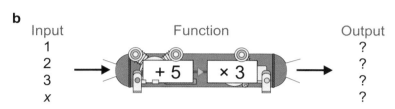

Input	Function	Output
1		?
2	+5 ×3	?
3		?
x		?

2 Find the inputs for this function machine:

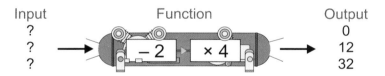

Input	Function	Output
?		0
?	–2 ×4	12
?		32

3 Draw a mapping diagram for this function machine:

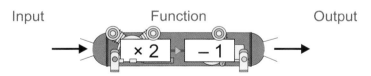

Input	Function	Output
	×2 –1	

Use 1, 2, 3, 4 as the inputs.

4 Write the function for the machine in question **3** using algebra: $x \rightarrow ...$

5 **a** What is the inverse of the function $x \rightarrow x + 3$?
  b Show the function and its inverse on a mapping diagram. Use 1, 2, 3, 4 as inputs.

6 Find the inverse of each of these functions:
  a $x \rightarrow 2x$ **b** $x \rightarrow 4x - 5$ **c** $x \rightarrow 3(x + 1)$

Coordinates

1 **a** Write down the coordinates of points A and D.

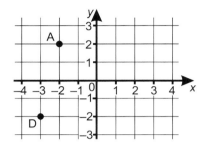

b Copy the diagram and plot the points B(1, 2) and C(2, –2).

c Join the four points. What shape have you drawn?

2 Write down the coordinates of the points A to J.

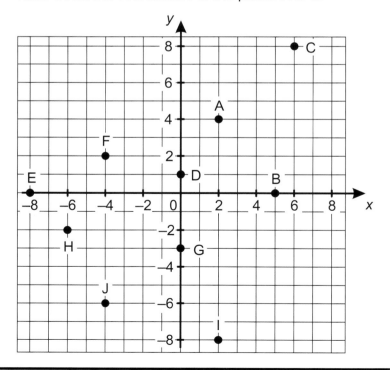

Straight-line graphs

1 a Copy and complete this table of values for the equation $y = 2x + 3$:

x	−3	−2	−1	0	1	2
y = 2x + 3	−3			3		

b Copy this grid and draw the graph of $y = 2x + 3$:

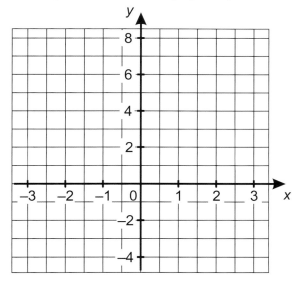

2 Find the gradient of each of these lines:

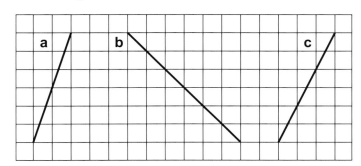

3 Does the line $y = 4x$ go through the point (7, 28)?
Explain how you know.

continued ⟶

Straight-line graphs (continued)

4 Match these equations to their graphs:

$$y = x, \ y = 4, \ x = 4, \ y = -x$$

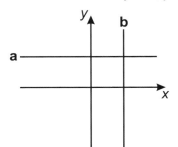

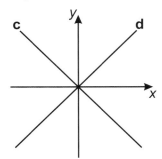

5 A straight line has a gradient of 2 and a y-intercept of –5. Which of these is the equation of the graph?
a $y = 2x + 5$ **b** $y = -5x + 2$ **c** $y = 2x - 5$

6 Write down the equation of the graph that has gradient 3 and goes through $(0, -1)$.

7 Are $y = 3x + 1$ and $y = 4x + 1$ parallel? How do you know?

 8 The straight line with equation $y = x + 2$ goes through the point $(-3, -1)$.
Copy this grid and draw the graph of $y = x + 2$.

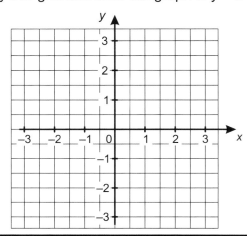

Real-life graphs

1 a £1 is roughly €1.40.
   Use this fact to copy and complete the table.

Amount in pounds	0	10	20	30	40	50
Amount in euros	0	14				

b Plot the points
   from your table
   on a grid like this:

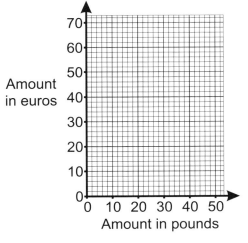

Amount in euros

Amount in pounds

2 The graph shows Jenny's cycle to and from a local shop.
   On her way home, she meets her sister, Susie.
   At this point Jenny gets off her bike and walks with Susie.
   Use the letters to explain what each part of the graph shows.

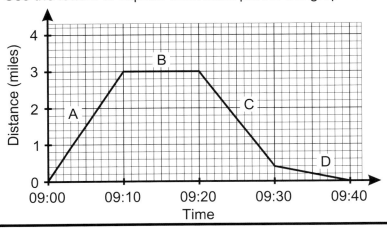

Inequalities

1   List the integer values of x that satisfy $-2 \leqslant x < 6$.

2   Everyone in the class got at least 40% in the test, but nobody scored 100%.
    Write this statement as an inequality.

3   Write the inequality shown on each number line:

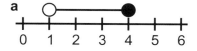

4   Show the inequality $x > -1$ on a number line.

5   Solve these inequalities.
    Show each solution on a number line.
    a $4x < 12$ b $2x + 1 \geqslant 5$ c $3x < x + 8$

Trial & improvement

1   The equation $x^2 + x = 10$ has a solution between 2 and 3.
    Use a table like this to find the solution using trial and improvement.
    Give your answer correct to 1 d.p.

x	$x^2 + x$	Comment
2	6	Too small
3	12	Too big

2   The equation $x^3 - x^2 = 35$ has a solution between 3 and 4.
    Use a table like this to find the solution using trial and improvement.
    Give your answer correct to 1 d.p.

x	$x^3 - x^2$	Comment
3	18	Too small
4	48	Too big

Units of measurement

1 How many:
  a centimetres in 10 m   **b** millimetres in 10 cm
  c metres in 100 km   **d** grams in 10 kg
  e millilitres in 100 litres?

2 How many:
  a inches in a foot   **b** feet in a yard
  c ounces in a pound   **d** pints in a gallon?

3 Roughly how many:
  a centimetres in a foot   **b** kilometres in a mile
  c grams in a pound   **d** grams in an ounce
  e pints in a litre?

4 Convert each of these measurements into centimetres:
  a 3 m   **b** 4 m   **c** 12 m
  d 23 m   **e** 19.6 m   **f** 0.75 m

5 Convert each of these measurements into millimetres:
  a 2 cm   **b** 5 cm   **c** 11 cm
  d 30.5 cm   **e** 76.7 cm   **f** 0.4 cm

6 Convert each of these measurements into metres:
  a 3 km   **b** 4 km   **c** 10 km
  d 23.4 km   **e** 50.25 km   **f** 0.8435 km

7 Convert each of these measurements:
  a 2 kg to grams   **b** 5 kg to grams
  c 15 kg to grams   **d** 3.5 litres to millilitres
  e 9.85 litres to millilitres   **f** 18.635 litres to millilitres

8 Convert each of these measurements:
  a 200 mm to centimetres   **b** 3000 m to kilometres
  c 800 cm to metres   **d** 5000 ml to litres
  e 7000 g to kilograms   **f** 14 000 ml to litres

9 Convert each of these measurements:
  a 45 mm to centimetres   **b** 400 g to kilograms
  c 6750 ml to litres   **d** 6.2 cm to millimetres
  e 1.54 m to centimetres   **f** 0.535 km to metres

Reading scales & accuracy

1 Write down the value shown on each of these scales:

a 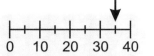   **b**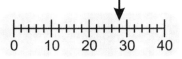

c 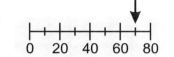   **d**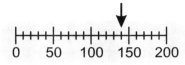

e    **f**

2 Tanya has measured the length of her garden as 4 m to the nearest metre.
Copy and complete the inequality to show the range of possible lengths of her garden:

   $3.5 \leqslant$ length (m) $<$ ....

3 David has weighed his bag as 6 kg to the nearest kilogram. What is the minimum that his bag could actually weigh?

4 Find the lower and upper limits for these measurements:
   a 11 cm to the nearest cm   **b** 20 km to the nearest km
   c 63 kg to the nearest kg   **d** 100 litres to the nearest litre
   e 19 m to the nearest m   **f** 5.4 cm to the nearest mm

Estimating & measuring angles

1 How many degrees are there in:
   a a quarter turn   **b** a half turn
   c a three-quarter turn   **d** a full turn?

2 For each of these angles:
   i first estimate its size
   ii then measure the angle.

a 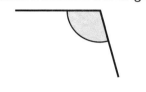   **b**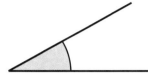

c    **d**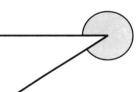

Angles & parallel lines

1 Which of these angles are acute, obtuse, reflex or right angles?

a    **b**

c 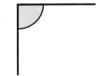   **d**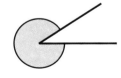

2 **a** What do the angles on a straight line add up to?
   b What do the angles around a point add up to?
   c What sort of angles are formed when two straight lines cross?

continued ⟶»

Angles & parallel lines (continued)

3 Find the size of the unknown angles:

a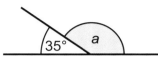
35° *a*

b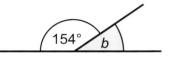
154° *b*

c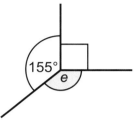
155° *e*

d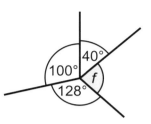
40°
100° *f*
128°

e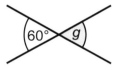
60° *g*

f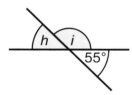
h *i*
55°

4 On a copy of the diagram, show:
   a the alternate angle to
   angle *P* (label it *A*)
   b the corresponding angle to
   angle *P* (label it *C*).

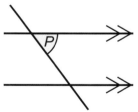
P

5 Find the size of the unknown angles:

a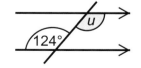
u
124°

b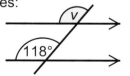
v
118°

c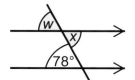
w
x
78°

d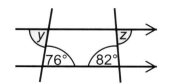
y *z*
76° 82°

Polygons

1 **a** What do the angles in a triangle add up to?
   b What do the angles in a quadrilateral add up to?

2 Find the size of the unknown angles:

a

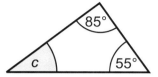

b

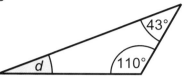

c

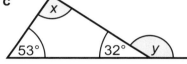

d

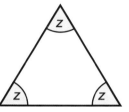

3 Find the size of the unknown angles:

a

b

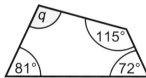

c

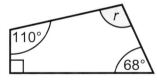

d

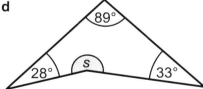

4 Complete these formulae for angles in a polygon:
   a Sum of exterior angles = ...°
   b Sum of interior angles = (number of sides – ......) × ....°

5 **a** How many interior angles does a hexagon have?
   b Calculate the size of an interior angle of a regular hexagon.
   c What is the size of an exterior angle of a regular hexagon?

Symmetry & properties of shapes

 1 Copy each shape and then draw its lines of symmetry.

a 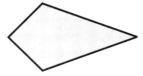 **b**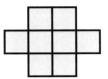

c   **d**

2 For each of these shapes:
   i write down the number of lines of symmetry
   ii state the order of rotation symmetry.

a   **b**

c 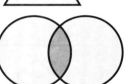 **d**

3 Which of these letters have:
   a reflection symmetry
   b rotation symmetry
   c no symmetry?

> A E F H
> M N P S
> T U W Z

4 How many planes of symmetry do these shapes have?

a   **b**

Equilateral triangular prism   Square-based pyramid

continued »»

Symmetry & properties of shapes (cont)

5 There are many ways that you can slice a cone:

Describe how to slice a cone so that the cross-section is an isosceles triangle.

6 Name these polygons:

a  **b**  **c**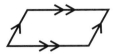

7 Copy and complete this table.

Name of polygon	Number of sides	All sides equal?	All angles equal?	Number of lines of symmetry	Order of rotation symmetry
Square					
Rectangle					
Isosceles triangle					
Equilateral triangle					
Rhombus					
Kite					
Trapezium					
Regular pentagon					
	4	No	No	0	2

Reflection

1 Reflect these shapes in the mirror lines:

a

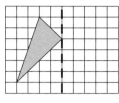

b

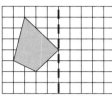

c

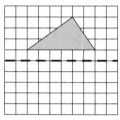

d

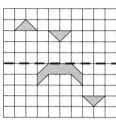

2 Reflect the shape in both mirror lines to make a symmetrical pattern:

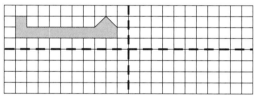

3 **a** Reflect triangle A in the line $x = 1$. Label the image B.

   b Triangle A is reflected on to triangle C. What is the equation of the mirror line?

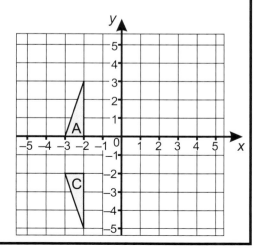

34

Rotation

 1 Rotate these shapes 90° clockwise about the dots:

a 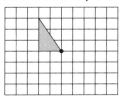   **b**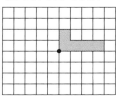

2 Rotate these shapes 90° anticlockwise about the dots:

a 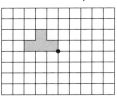   **b**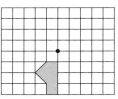

3 Rotate these shapes 180° about the dots:

a 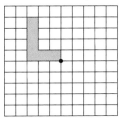   **b**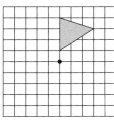

4 **a** Rotate shape A 90° anticlockwise about the origin.
Label the image B.

  b Shape A is rotated 90° clockwise on to shape C.
Find the coordinates of the centre of rotation.

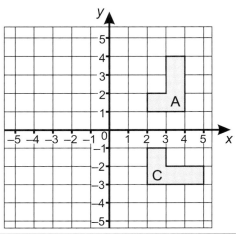

Translation

 1 Translate these shapes 3 squares to the right and 2 down.

a 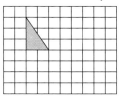 **b**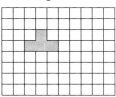

2 Translate these shapes 4 squares to the left and 3 down.

a 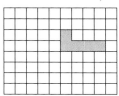 **b**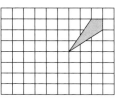

3 Translate these shapes 5 squares to the left and 4 up.

a 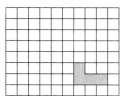 **b**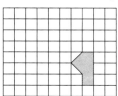

4 Describe these translations:
  a A to B
  b B to C
  c C to D
  d D to E
  e E to F
  f F to G
  g G to H
  h H to I

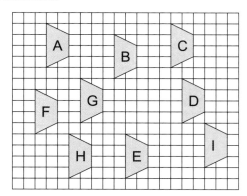

Speedy Revision

Enlargement

1 Copy these diagrams on to squared paper.
Enlarge each shape by scale factor 2 with centre C.

a   **b**   **c**

2 Copy these diagrams on to squared paper.
Enlarge each shape by scale factor 3 with centre C.

a   **b**   **c**

3 In these diagrams, shape B is an enlargement of shape A.
Find the scale factor of each enlargement.

a 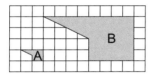 **b**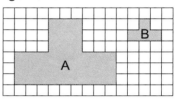

4 **a** On a copy of the diagram, enlarge shape A with scale
factor 0.5 and centre (–2, 3). Label the image B.

b Shape D is an
enlargement of
shape C.
Find the scale factor
and the coordinates
of the centre of this
enlargement.

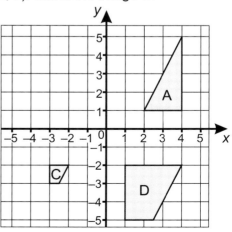

           Tier 5–7

Perimeter & circumference

1 Find the perimeter of each of these shapes.

a
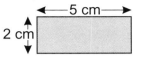
2 cm — 5 cm

b
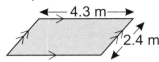
4.3 m — 2.4 m

2 Find the perimeter of each of these shapes:

a
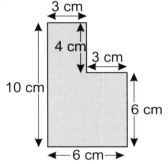
3 cm, 4 cm, 3 cm, 10 cm, 6 cm, 6 cm

b
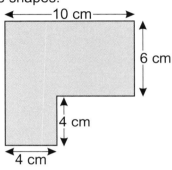
10 cm, 6 cm, 4 cm, 4 cm

c
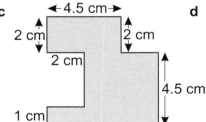
4.5 cm, 2 cm, 2 cm, 2 cm, 4.5 cm, 1 cm, 6.5 cm

d
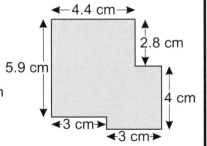
4.4 cm, 2.8 cm, 5.9 cm, 4 cm, 3 cm, 3 cm

3 Find the circumference of each of these circles:

a

6 cm

b

9.4 cm

c

4 cm

4 Find the perimeter of each of these shapes:

a

5 cm

b
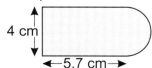
4 cm, 5.7 cm

Areas of triangles & quadrilaterals

1 Write down the formula for each of these:
- **a** the area of a triangle
- **b** the area of a parallelogram
- **c** the area of a trapezium

2 Find the area of each of these shapes.
Remember to state the units of your answer.

a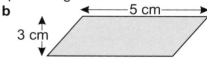

b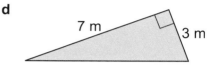

c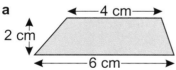

d

3 Find the area of each of these parallelograms:

a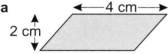

b

4 Find the area of each of these trapeziums:

a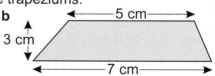

b

5 Find the area of each of these shapes:

a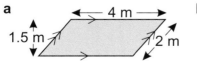

b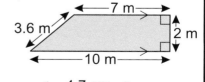

c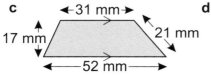

d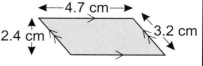

Areas of circles & composite shapes

1 Find the area of each of these circles:

a
5 cm

b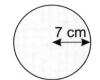
7 cm

c
←5.7 m→

2 Find the area of each of these shapes:

a
←5 cm→

b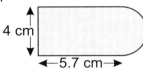
4 cm
←5.7 cm→

c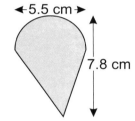
←5.5 cm→
7.8 cm

d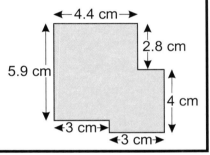
←4.4 cm→
2.8 cm
5.9 cm
4 cm
←3 cm→
←3 cm→

More circles

1 For each of these circles calculate:
   i the length of the grey arc
   ii the area of the grey sector.

a
4 cm

b
3.1 m
135°

c
8.1 cm
225°

2 B and D are points on the circle.
AB and AD are tangents to the circle.
C is the centre of the circle.
Angle BAD is 38°.
Work out the size of angle BCD.

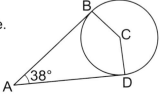
B
C
A 38°
D

Pythagoras' theorem

1 Find the length of the hypotenuse in each of these triangles.
Give your answers to 1 decimal place where appropriate.

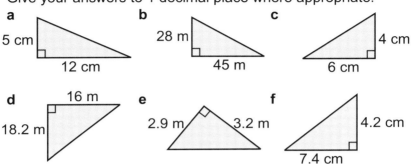

a 5 cm, 12 cm

b 28 m, 45 m

c 4 cm, 6 cm

d 16 m, 18.2 m

e 2.9 m, 3.2 m

f 4.2 cm, 7.4 cm

2 Find the missing lengths for each of these triangles.
Give your answers to 1 decimal place where appropriate.

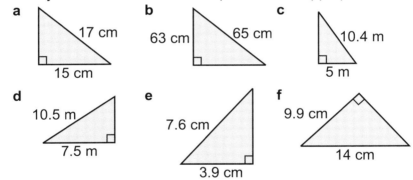

a 17 cm, 15 cm

b 63 cm, 65 cm

c 10.4 m, 5 m

d 10.5 m, 7.5 m

e 7.6 cm, 3.9 cm

f 9.9 cm, 14 cm

3 Navinder walks 3 km due south and then 7 km due east.
Calculate the distance that Navinder is from his starting
position.

4 The base of a ladder is 1.5 m from the base of a wall on level
ground. The ladder reaches 3 m up the wall.
Find the length of the ladder.

5 Find the distance between each pair of points:
   a (0, 0) and (3, 4)   **b** (2, 3) and (9, 27)
   c (2, 4) and (23, 24)   **d** (4, 5) and (6, 9)
   e (−2, −5) and (3, 7)   **f** (−5, 2) and (4, −3)

Nets & 3-D shapes; plans & elevations

1 Which of these nets will fold to make a cube?

  a   **b** 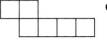   **c**

2 Name the 3-D shapes that these nets make:

  a   **b**   **c**

3 Sketch a net for each of these shapes:

  a   **b**   **c**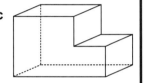

4 For each of these shapes, draw a front elevation, a side elevation and a plan view.

  a 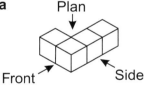   **b**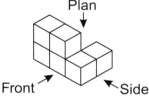

  c 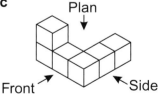   **d**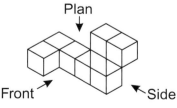

5 Here are the three views of two solid shapes.
Draw each shape on isometric paper.

  a
      Plan   Front   Side

  b
      Plan   Front   Side

Volume & surface area

1 Find the volume of each of these shapes:

a 2.2 cm   2.2 cm
1.4 cm

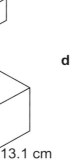

b

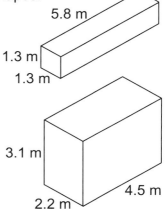

5.8 m
1.3 m
1.3 m

c

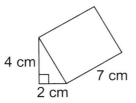

12 cm
15.4 cm   13.1 cm

d

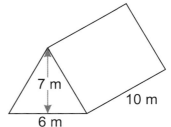

3.1 m
2.2 m   4.5 m

2 For each triangular prism find:
i the area of the triangular end
ii the volume of the prism.

a

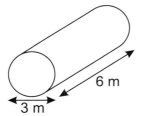

4 cm
7 cm
2 cm

b

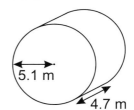

7 m
6 m
10 m

3 The area of the cross-section
of this prism is 24 m².
Find the volume of the prism.

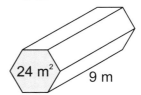

24 m²   9 m

4 Find the volume of each of these cylinders.

a

6 m
3 m

b

5.1 m
4.7 m

continued ⟶»

Volume & surface area (continued)

5 These shapes are made with centimetre cubes.
Find the surface area of each shape.

a  **b** 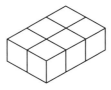 **c**

6 Find the surface area of these shapes:

a  2.2 cm — 2.2 cm — 1.4 cm

b 5.8 m — 1.3 m — 1.3 m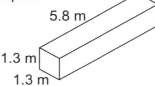

c 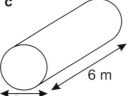 6 m — 3 m

d 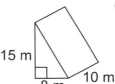 15 m — 8 m — 10 m

e 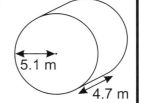 5.1 m — 4.7 m

7 The surface area of a cube is 96 m².
Find the length of a side of the cube.

8 A cylinder has a volume of 300 m³. Its radius is 5 m.
Find the length of the cylinder.

9 Change the units of these areas to cm².
a 4 m² **b** 10 m² **c** 0.5 m²

10 Change the units of these areas to m².
a 3000 cm² **b** 20 000 cm² **c** 100 cm²

11 Change the units of these volumes to cm³.
a 4 m³ **b** 25 m³ **c** 0.02 m³

12 Change the units of these volumes to m³.
a 7 000 000 cm³ **b** 75 000 000 cm³ **c** 40 000 cm³

44

Bearings & scale drawings

1 Use a protractor to find the bearing of B from A in each of these diagrams:

a

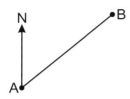

b

2 A map has a scale of 1 cm = 50 km.
How far in real life are these lengths on the map?
a 3 cm **b** 5 cm **c** 2.5 mm

3 A diagram is drawn using a scale of 1 cm represents 20 cm.
How long on the diagram would these real-life lengths be?
a 40 cm **b** 10 cm **c** 8 mm

4 The following diagram is drawn using a scale of 1 cm to represent 2 km.

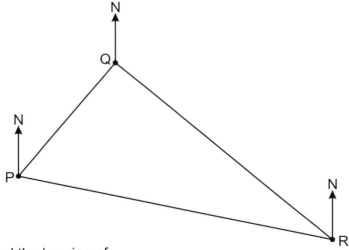

Find the bearing of:
a R from Q **b** Q from P **c** P from Q.

Find the distance from:
d P to Q **e** P to R **f** Q to R.

Compound measures

1 Work out the average speed (in km/h) of a car that travels:

  a 230 km in 4 hours   **b** 425 km in 5 hours

  c 36 km in 30 minutes   **d** 15 km in 10 minutes

2 A bus travels at 45 mph.
Find how far the bus will travel in:

  a 3 hours   **b** 12 minutes

Find how long the bus will take to travel:

  c 315 miles   **d** 60 miles

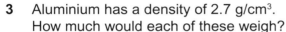

3 Aluminium has a density of 2.7 g/cm^3.
How much would each of these weigh?

  a 20 cm^3 of aluminium   **b** 1 m^3 of aluminium

Find the volume of these:

  c 81 g of aluminium   **d** 1 kg of aluminium

Constructions & loci

1 Copy the diagram and construct the perpendicular bisector of the line AB. Clearly show your construction marks.

    A•————————————————•B

                   7 cm

2 Using a ruler and compasses construct an equilateral triangle with sides of 5 cm.

3 The road between Milton and Newham is 8 km long and completely straight.

    Milton•————————————•Newham

                  8 km

  a Draw a scale diagram of the road using a scale of 1 cm to 1 km.

  b Using compasses find the midpoint of the road between Milton and Newham. Clearly show your construction marks.

continued →»

Constructions & loci (continued)

4 Dave stands on a line.
He kicks a football on a
path perpendicular to the line.

Copy the diagram below and
construct a line to show the
path of the ball.

———————————•———————————
Ball

5 A goat is tethered to a post with
a 10 m piece of rope.

Draw a plan diagram to show
the region that the goat can reach.
Use a scale of 1 cm to 2 m.

6 In a garden, the South wall is perpendicular to the East wall.

There is a path in the garden
such that anyone who walks
along it is always the same
distance from the South wall
as the East wall.

Draw a diagram to show the
position of the path.

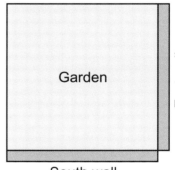

Garden

East wall

South wall

7 *Hurry Curry* will deliver takeaways within a 4 mile radius.
Tandoori Express will deliver within a 3 mile radius.
The takeaway restaurants are 5 miles apart.

Hurry Curry •◄——————————►• Tandoori Express
              5 miles

Draw a diagram, using a scale of 2 cm to 1 mile, to show the
region that both takeaway restaurants deliver to.

Mean, median, mode, range

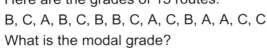

1   Cycling routes are graded A, B or C.
    Here are the grades of 15 routes:

    B, C, A, B, C, B, B, C, A, C, B, A, A, C, C

    What is the modal grade?

2   Find the mode for each of these sets of data:
    a   Days in first 6 months: 31, 28, 31, 30, 31, 30
    b   Hours spent driving: 4, 3, 4, 2, 3, 4, 2, 1, 2, 3, 3, 2, 2

3   Find the median for each of these sets of data:
    a   Number of pens: 7, 8, 4, 6, 2, 5, 4
    b   Hours of sunshine: 4, 7, 2, 5, 7, 4, 1, 6

4   Find the mean for each of these sets of data:
    a   Number of cars in a car park: 12, 32, 18, 15, 34
    b   Pocket money: £5, £4, £2.50, £3, £9.50, £3, £15

5   Find the range for each of these sets of data:
    a   Dress sizes: 8, 14, 12, 10, 18, 8, 8, 10, 12, 12, 16
    b   Number of ants: 124, 200, 25, 32, 255
    c   Mass of parcels in kilograms: 10, 4.5, 14.5, 5, 13.5, 7

6   Find the mean, median, mode and range for each of these
    sets of data:
    a   Length of copper pipe in metres: 3, 4, 4, 6, 2, 3, 2.5
    b   Water in a cup in millilitres: 12, 12.3, 17.4, 12.3, 14, 20.6
    c   Carrots in a bag: 23, 31, 15, 12, 23, 5, 17
    d   Weight in kilograms: 65.4, 68.2, 69.2, 68.3, 65.3, 62.6

7   The frequency table shows the number of cars per
    household in Carrie's street.

Number of cars	0	1	2	3
Frequency	3	6	4	2

    Find the mean number of cars per household.

8   Jerome received a mean of 2.4 text messages per day last
    month, with a range of 5 − 0 = 5. Kay received a mean of 1.9
    per day last month, with a range of 3 − 1 = 2.
    Which of them is more likely to get a text message today?

Collecting data & two-way tables

1   Jenny would like to know people's opinions about her local
    swimming pool. She designs the following questionnaire:

Question 1	How often do you go swimming? Never ☐, occasionally ☐, frequently ☐
Question 2	Do you agree that the swimming pool is good value for money? Yes ☐, no ☐
Question 3	How much do you earn per year? £9999 or less ☐, £10 000 to £19 999 ☐, £20 000 to £29 999 ☐, £30 000 or more ☐

Jenny's teacher says that all of her questions need changing.
a State a fault for each question.

Jenny intends to conduct her survey outside the swimming
pool on a Monday morning.
b Give two reasons why this is unsuitable.

2   Explain the difference between primary and secondary data.

3   For each part of question **6** on the previous page (page 48)
    state whether the data is discrete or continuous.

4   Complete the two-way table that shows the number of MP3
    and MP4 players owned by a group of friends.

	MP3	MP4	Total
Boys own	15		
Girls own		3	
Total	32		41

5   Complete the two-way table that shows the colours and
    brands (Trek or Giant) of some racing bikes in a cycle shop.

	Red	Blue	Silver	Total
Trek	3			9
Giant		6	4	
Total	8		6	

Frequency tables

1 Sandy has noted down the colours of 20 revision books.
Here is her data:

yellow, orange, purple, purple, purple, orange, orange,
yellow, purple, orange, purple, yellow, purple, purple, yellow,
purple, orange, purple, yellow, purple

Draw a frequency table to show her data.

2 Liam counted the number of potatoes in 20 bags.
Here are his results:

29, 35, 42, 46, 34, 48, 28, 33, 43, 39,
27, 30, 44, 52, 45, 51, 39, 40, 38, 51

  a Copy and complete this frequency table for the data.

Number of potatoes	Tally	Frequency
26 to 35		
36 to 45		
46 to 55		
Total		

  b Re-draw the frequency table using the intervals:
  $20 \leqslant N < 30$, $30 \leqslant N < 40$, $40 \leqslant N < 50$, $50 \leqslant N < 60$,
  where N is the number of potatoes.

3 Here are the test scores of 17 students:

5, 25, 43, 55, 23, 12, 37, 54, 32, 4, 17, 16, 34, 21, 43, 38, 28

Draw a grouped frequency table for the data, using the
intervals: $0 \leqslant S < 10$, $10 \leqslant S < 20$, etc.

4 The table shows the weights
of some suitcases.

  a Estimate the mean weight
  of a suitcase.

  b Which group contains the
  median weight?

  c Which is the modal group?

Weight (W kg)	Frequency
$0 \leqslant W < 6$	2
$6 \leqslant W < 12$	5
$12 \leqslant W < 18$	7
$18 \leqslant W < 24$	10
$24 \leqslant W < 30$	3

Bar charts & frequency diagrams

1 The bar chart shows
the number of medals
that Middlehampton
School won in a
swimming competition.

How many medals did
the school win in total?

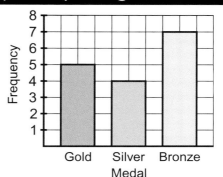

2 Draw a bar chart to represent the data in the table below.

Make of car	Honda	Ford	Nissan	BMW
Frequency	5	8	6	3

3 The table shows the weights
of some letters.

Draw a frequency diagram
to show the data.

Weight (W g)	Frequency
$0 \leqslant W < 10$	1
$10 \leqslant W < 20$	3
$20 \leqslant W < 30$	5
$30 \leqslant W < 40$	6
$40 \leqslant W < 50$	2

4 The table shows the lengths
of some pieces of wood.

a Draw a frequency diagram
to show the data.
b Draw a frequency polygon
to show the data.

Length (L cm)	Frequency
$0 \leqslant L < 50$	4
$50 \leqslant L < 100$	3
$100 \leqslant L < 150$	9
$150 \leqslant L < 200$	7
$200 \leqslant L < 250$	4

5 The table shows the volumes
of some cuboids.

Draw a frequency polygon
to show the data.

Volume (V cm³)	Frequency
$0 \leqslant V < 25$	24
$25 \leqslant V < 50$	56
$50 \leqslant V < 75$	44
$75 \leqslant V < 100$	32
$100 \leqslant V < 125$	18

Stem & leaf diagrams; line graphs

1 Here are the heights of 23 people in centimetres.

131, 136, 138, 143, 146, 148, 153, 154, 155, 158, 159, 160, 162, 164, 165, 167, 168, 170, 171, 173, 178, 184, 187

Copy and complete the stem and leaf diagram for the data:

130	1
140	
150	
160	0 2
170	
180	

Key:

130	1

represents 131 cm

2 Here are the weights of 23 people in kilograms.

61, 67, 84, 93, 72, 57, 65, 86, 49, 63, 75, 69, 76, 69, 46, 70, 56, 71, 53, 48, 52, 54, 64

a Draw a stem and leaf diagram for the data.
Use multiples of 10 as the stems and units as the leaves.

b Use your diagram to find the median weight.

3 The graph shows the amount of water in a barrel over the course of a year.

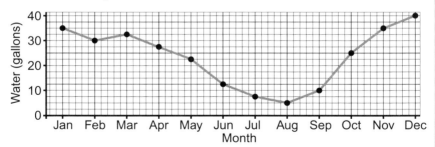

a How much water was in the barrel in May?

b In which months were there 35 gallons of water in the barrel?

c Between which two months was the greatest increase in the amount of water in the barrel?

d Describe any trends you can see in the graph.

Pie charts

1 The pie chart shows the favourite type of chocolate of 32 women.
   a How many of the women prefer plain chocolate?
   b How many of the women prefer white chocolate?

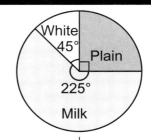

2 The pie chart shows the results of a survey of how 24 students spend their Saturday mornings.
   a How many students watch TV?
   b How many students shop?
   c How many students work?

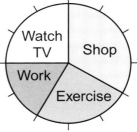

3 The table below shows the colours of 24 pairs of jeans:

Colour	Stonewash	Black	Untreated	Glitter
Frequency	3	7	10	4
Angle				

   a By copying and completing the table above, draw a pie chart to show the colours of the jeans.
   b What fraction of the jeans are untreated?
      Give your answer as a fraction in its lowest terms.

4 Here is the nutritional information for a 120 g jar of gravy granules:

Nutritional information	120 g
Protein	12 g
Carbohydrate	60 g
Fat	40 g
Sodium	8 g

Draw a pie chart to show the nutritional information.

Scatter graphs

1   Nisha has collected some data that shows that the hotter the weather the more ice-creams are sold.
    Which of these scatter graphs represents her data?

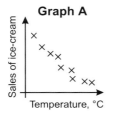
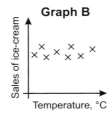
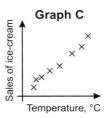

Graph A   **Graph B**   **Graph C**

2   The table shows how far some people live from a cinema, and how often they went to the cinema last year.

Distance (km)	17	3	11	1	7	14	9	6
Number of visits	0	26	14	35	16	2	12	24

a   Show the data as a scatter diagram.
b   Describe the correlation for the data.

3   The table shows the results of 10 students taking 2 tests.

Test 1	16	40	6	20	9	31	46	44	24	32
Test 2	16	32	6	22	18	26	44	36	28	34

a   Draw a scatter graph for the data.
b   Draw a line of best fit on your diagram.
c   Pru scored 30 on Test 1, but missed Test 2 through illness. Use your line of best fit to estimate the score Pru would have got on Test 2.

4   The table shows the value and age of some motorbikes.

Age (years)	4	1	8	3	4	7	6	2
Value (£000s)	7	13	3	11	12	7	3	19

a   Show the data as a scatter graph.
b   Describe the correlation for the data.
c   Draw a line of best fit on your graph.
d   Estimate the value of a 5-year-old motorbike.

Speedy Revision

Probability

1 Copy this probability line:

Impossible ——+——————+——————+—— Certain

Show these events on your line:
a The next baby born is a girl.
b A horse passing a driving test.
c You will drink something tomorrow.
d Picking a Spade from a pack of ordinary playing cards.

2 A letter is picked at random from the word PRINTER.
a What is the probability that the letter is T?
b What is the probability that the letter is R?

3 A bag contains 3 red marbles and 7 blue marbles.
A marble is drawn at random from the bag.
a Find the probability that the marble is red.
b What is the probability that the marble is green?

4 A normal fair dice is thrown. Find the probability of getting:
a a 3   **b** an odd number   **c** a 4 or a 5.

5 A 3-sided spinner is spun 100 times, with these results:

Colour	Purple	Red	Blue
Frequency	60	25	15

The spinner is spun one more time.
Estimate the probability of the spinner landing on:
a red   **b** purple.

6 The probability of winning a prize is 0.15.
What is the probability of not winning a prize?

7 What does the probability of it raining and the probability of it not raining add up to?

8 Daisy always wears jeans and a T-shirt.
The table shows the colours of her jeans and T-shirts.

Jeans	T-shirts
Black	Red
Blue	Yellow
White	Pink

a List all the possible combinations of jeans and T-shirts she could wear.
b The probability of her wearing the red T-shirt is 0.78.
What is the probability of her not wearing the red T-shirt?

Answers

Page 4 Special numbers
1 **a** Square numbers; 16, 36, 49, 81
b Triangular numbers; 15, 21, 45, 55
2 2, 3, 5, 7, 11, 13, 17, 19, 23, 29
3 **a** 43, 17, 23 **b** 25, 64, 36 **c** 10, 36

Page 4 Multiples, factors & prime factors
1 **a** 9, 18, 27, 36, 45 **b** 4, 8, 12, 16, 20
c 10, 20, 30, 40, 50 **d** 7, 14, 21, 28, 35
e 6, 12, 18, 24, 30 **f** 11, 22, 33, 44, 55
g 3, 6, 9, 12, 15 **h** 20, 40, 60, 80, 100
2 **a** True **b** True **c** False **d** False
e True **f** False **g** False **h** True
3 **a** 1, 3, 9, 27 **b** 1, 2, 7, 14
c 1, 2, 3, 4, 6, 9, 12, 18, 36
d 1, 2, 4, 5, 10, 20
e 1, 2, 4, 5, 10, 20, 25, 50, 100
f 1, 3, 7, 9, 21, 63 **g** 1, 7, 49
h 1, 2, 4, 11, 22, 44
4 **a** 1, 47; prime **b** 1, 3, 17, 51; not prime
c 1, 3, 13, 39; not prime **d** 1, 37; prime
5 **a** 3, 18, 12 **b** 32, 12
6 **a** $2 \times 2 \times 7 = 2^2 \times 7$ **b** $3 \times 5 \times 7$
c $2 \times 3 \times 3 \times 3 = 2 \times 3^3$ **d** $2 \times 3 \times 13$
e $2 \times 2 \times 5 \times 5 = 2^2 \times 5^2$
f 2×23 **g** $2 \times 2 \times 5 \times 7 = 2^2 \times 5 \times 7$
h $2 \times 3 \times 3 \times 5 = 2 \times 3^2 \times 5$
7 686

Page 5 LCM & HCF
1 **a** 9 **b** 40 **c** 24 **d** 48 **e** 105 **f** 42
g 200 **h** 150
2 **a** 6 **b** 5 **c** 12 **d** 7 **e** 16 **f** 1 **g** 14 **h** 15
3 75 minutes later, at 10:15

Page 5 Mult' & div' by 10, 100, 1000, ...
1 **a** 540 **b** 9000 **c** 500 **d** 63 **e** 80 **f** 200
g 32 **h** 45 **i** 50.6
2 **a** 4 **b** 9.6 **c** 20 **d** 31.9 **e** 2.48 **f** 0.71
g 1.11 **h** 41.6 **i** 5.1
3 **a** 5400 **b** 770 **c** 24 000 **d** 21 000
e 2000 **f** 1.8 **g** 10.69 **h** 0.27 **i** 0.026
4 **a** 40 **b** 0.4 **c** 11 **d** 0.3 **e** 80 **f** 0.19
g 108 **h** 219 **i** 5.7

Page 6 Rounding
1 **a** 30 **b** 70 **c** 1070 **d** 240 **e** 4020 **f** 50
g 28 560 **h** 10
2 **a** 500 **b** 800 **c** 100 **d** 0 **e** 1300 **f** 5000
g 20 700 **h** 300
3 **a** 2000 **b** 5000 **c** 1000 **d** 0 **e** 12 000
f 7000 **g** 7000 **h** 31 000

4 **a** 1 **b** 3 **c** 11 **d** 1 **e** 8 **f** 1 **g** 12 **h** 17
5 **a** 6.2 **b** 0.6 **c** 1.4 **d** 2.7 **e** 3.8 **f** 24.8
g 7.1 **h** 301.6
6 **a** 1.44 **b** 9.03 **c** 4.94 **d** 10.84 **e** 0.61
f 2.99 **g** 12.10 **h** 1.72
7 **a** 30 000 **b** 10 **c** 0.1 **d** 2000
8 **a** 0.99 **b** 2.1 **c** 210 **d** 28 000
9 **a** 1240 **b** 0.705 **c** 33 300 **d** 9.61
10 $3 \times 5 = 15$ cm   11 $3 \times 2^2 = 12$ cm^2

Page 7 Fractions
1 **a** $\frac{2}{8} = \frac{1}{4}$ **b** $\frac{3}{9} = \frac{1}{3}$ **c** $\frac{3}{12} = \frac{1}{4}$ **d** $\frac{2}{6} = \frac{1}{3}$
e $\frac{6}{12} = \frac{3}{4} = \frac{1}{2}$ **f** $\frac{12}{48} = \frac{6}{24} = \frac{4}{16} = \frac{3}{12} = \frac{2}{8} = \frac{1}{4}$
2 **a** $\frac{1}{2}$ **b** $\frac{1}{2}$ **c** $\frac{2}{5}$ **d** $\frac{1}{7}$ **e** $\div 5$
f $\div 4$, $\frac{2}{3}$
3 **a** $\frac{3}{4}$ **b** $\frac{1}{6}$ **c** $\frac{1}{3}$ **d** $\frac{1}{6}$ **e** $\frac{1}{3}$
f $\frac{1}{4}$ **g** $\frac{3}{5}$ **h** $\frac{1}{10}$ **i** $\frac{1}{4}$
4 **a** $\frac{3}{2}$ **b** $\frac{4}{3}$ **c** $\frac{7}{4}$ **d** $\frac{7}{5}$ **e** $\frac{13}{6}$
f $\frac{17}{7}$ **g** $\frac{21}{8}$ **h** $\frac{31}{10}$ **i** $\frac{29}{9}$
5 **a** $3\frac{2}{3}$ **b** $6\frac{1}{2}$ **c** $4\frac{1}{6}$ **d** $3\frac{2}{5}$ **e** $2\frac{2}{9}$
f $5\frac{1}{4}$ **g** $2\frac{1}{2}$ **h** $2\frac{3}{8}$ **i** $3\frac{1}{7}$
6 **a** $\frac{3}{8}$ **b** $\frac{5}{6}$ **c** $\frac{1}{2}$ **d** $1\frac{1}{2}$ **e** $\frac{7}{8}$
f $\frac{4}{5}$ **g** $\frac{5}{6}$ **h** $\frac{17}{35}$ **i** $1\frac{5}{12}$
7 **a** $\frac{1}{9}$ **b** $\frac{1}{6}$ **c** $\frac{3}{10}$ **d** $\frac{1}{6}$ **e** $\frac{2}{5}$
f $\frac{7}{8}$ **g** $\frac{5}{8}$ **h** $\frac{5}{12}$ **i** $\frac{1}{20}$
8 **a** $\frac{1}{2}$, $\frac{2}{3}$, $\frac{9}{12}$ **b** $\frac{4}{9}$, $\frac{11}{18}$, $\frac{2}{3}$ **c** $\frac{3}{5}$, $\frac{13}{20}$, $\frac{3}{4}$
9 **a** £30 **b** £30 × 2 = £60
10 **a** 25 m **b** 25 m × 3 = 75 m
11 **a** 7 mm **b** 7 mm × 2 = 14 mm
12 **a** 4p **b** 4p × 7 = 28p
13 240°   14 30 g
15 **a** $\frac{1}{6}$ **b** $\frac{2}{15}$ **c** $\frac{2}{7}$ **d** $\frac{1}{4}$
e $\frac{1}{10}$ **f** $\frac{2}{9}$
16 **a** $\frac{2}{3}$ **b** $\frac{7}{10}$ **c** $\frac{4}{15}$ **d** $\frac{14}{15}$
e 10 **f** $\frac{10}{3} = 3\frac{1}{3}$

Page 9 Percentages
1 40%   2 25%   3 30%
4 **a** 216 ml **b** £145.50 **c** 6 g
d 18 mm **e** £94.50 **f** 1.77 m
5 £4.38
6 **a** 33p **b** 18 mm **c** 126 g **d** 82 m
e £62.40 **f** 58.5 litres

Speedy Revision

Answers

Page 9 Percentages (cont)
7 **a** 63p **b** 57 mm **c** £23.52 **d** 119 g
e £18 400 **f** 49.95 litres
8 £9.60   9 105 mm
10 £241.50   11 £104.58

Page 10 Fractions, decimals & percentages
1 **a** 0.01 **b** 0.125 **c** 0.6 **d** 0.875 **e** 0.15
f 0.54 **g** 0.333... **h** 0.3

2 **a** $\frac{17}{100}$ **b** $\frac{23}{100}$ **c** $\frac{3}{100}$ **d** $\frac{129}{100} = 1\frac{29}{100}$
e $\frac{30}{100} = \frac{3}{10}$ **f** $\frac{75}{100} = \frac{3}{4}$
g $\frac{15}{100} = \frac{3}{20}$ **h** $\frac{112}{100} = 1\frac{3}{25}$

3 **a** 5% **b** 62% **c** 118% **d** 294% **e** 30%
f $33\frac{1}{3}$% **g** 80% **h** 150%

4 **a** 0.4 **b** 0.25 **c** 0.9 **d** 0.6 **e** 0.05 **f** 0.18
g 0.032 **h** 1.99

5 **a** $\frac{5}{10} = \frac{1}{2}$ **b** $\frac{1}{10}$ **c** $\frac{75}{100} = \frac{3}{4}$ **d** $\frac{7}{10}$
e $\frac{6}{10} = \frac{3}{5}$ **f** $\frac{13}{100}$ **g** $\frac{49}{100}$ **h** $\frac{45}{100} = \frac{9}{20}$

6 $\frac{2}{5}$ of £40 (= £16, 25% of £60 = £15)

7 **a** 27%, 0.5, $\frac{2}{3}$, 80%
b 39.9%, 0.51, $\frac{41}{10}$, $4\frac{1}{2}$
c 8.6%, 18%, 0.75, $\frac{20}{3}$

8 **b**   9 **c**   10 **a**

Page 11 Ratio & proportion
1 **a** $\frac{2}{6} = \frac{1}{3}$ **b** 67% **c** 2 : 4 = 1 : 2
2 8 : 7   3 3 : 2   4 1 : 2 : 3
5 **a** 2 : 5 **b** 4 : 5 : 25 **c** 9 : 2 **d** 2 : 3
e 40 : 13 **f** 7 : 10 **g** 7 : 6 **h** 7 : 10
i 1 : 4
6 160 ml
7 35°, 45°, 100°
8 31.25%
9 £1.05
10 £6
11 £2.88
12 280 g
13 **a** 24 : 25 **b** 165 : 175 = 33 : 35
14 90 : 36 = 5 : 2

Page 12 Negative numbers
1 **a** −3, −1, 1, 2, 4 **b** 3
2 7°C
3 **a** −6 **b** 10 **c** 8 **d** −30 **e** −21 **f** −9
g −2 **h** 3 **i** −15 **j** −1 **k** −3 **l** 16
4 **a** 4 **b** 13

Page 13 Powers & roots
1 **a** 49 **b** 125 **c** 1000 **d** 1 **e** 16 **f** 729
g 1 **h** $\frac{1}{5}$
2 **a** 529 **b** 512 **c** 625 **d** 4 **e** 1331
f 1024 **g** 0.0625 **h** 1.331
3 **a** 4 **b** 5 **c** 4 **d** 10
4 **a** 15 **b** 20 **c** 41 **d** 0.3
5 **a** 12.04 **b** 0.84 **c** 2 **d** 10.8
6 **a** 3^6 **b** 4^2 **c** 2^{11} **d** 3^8 **e** 7^4 **f** 12^{15}
g 9^5 **h** 15^3

Page 13 Standard index form
1 **a** 10^2 **b** 10^{-1} **c** 10^{-2} **d** 10^4
2 **a** 600 **b** 4000 **c** 26 000 **d** 380 000
e 0.67 **f** 0.083
3 **a** 2.1×10^2 **b** 3.8×10^3 **c** 4.5×10^2
d 6×10^{-1} **e** 9×10^{-2} **f** 1.7×10^2
4 4.8×10^3 g
5 9 460 000 000 000 km
6 **a** 0.21 **b** 1.8×10^4

Page 14 Written methods
1 **a** 2.78 **b** 39.9 **c** 7.97 **d** 10.52 **e** 9.15
f 9.17 **g** 5.27 **h** 68.2
2 **a** 1.84 **b** 4.11 **c** 2.12 **d** 4.19 **e** 7.62
f 19.44 **g** 7.19 **h** 230.92
3 **a** 273 **b** 378 **c** 442 **d** 714 **e** 672 **f** 2528
g 2280 **h** 3856
4 **a** 18.2 **b** 24.6 **c** 29.6 **d** 24.5 **e** 27.54
f 10.32 **g** 16.17 **h** 24.72
5 **a** 42 **b** 19 **c** 27 **d** 17 **e** 49 **f** 26
g 18 remainder 2 **h** 23 remainder 2
i 17 remainder 3 **j** 41 remainder 1
k 20 remainder 4 **l** 31 remainder 1
6 **a** 1.8 **b** 2.5 **c** 13.1 **d** 11.6 **e** 21.9 **f** 16.8
g 55 **h** 20.4
7 £106.42   8 £16.45   9 £14.20

Page 15 Calculations with brackets
1 **a** 20 **b** 40 **c** 4 **d** 11 **e** 198 **f** 64
g 212.905 **h** −0.53 **i** 5 **j** 7.39
2 **a** 8 × (4 + 6) = 80 **b** (3 + 8) × 12 = 132
c 36 ÷ (6 + 3) = 4 **d** Not needed
e 7 × (8 − 3) ÷ 5 = 7 **f** Not needed
g (8 + 7 − 3) × 4 = 48
h (−3 + 5) × (8 + 4) = 24
3 **a** 14 ÷ 2 = 7 **b** 18 ÷ 9 = 2
c 24 ÷ 8 = 3 **d** 32 ÷ 4 = 8
4 **a** 6.27 **b** 1.77 **c** 3.14 **d** 8.89
5 **a** 10.3 **b** 14.6

Answers

Page 16 Using letters

1 **a** $8s + 6$ **b** $5a + 6$ **c** $4n + 2$ **d** $7m + 2$
   e $7b + 2$ **f** $7c + 3$ **g** $8t + 7$ **h** $4g + 8$
   i $2n + 9$ **j** $-3 - 2y$
2 **a** $6x + 4$ **b** $8x + 4$ **c** $9x - 2$ **d** $9x - 1$
3 **a** $2x + 2$ **b** $3x + 5$
4 **a** $\frac{2x}{5}$ **b** $\frac{2x}{3}$ **c** $\frac{3x}{8}$ **d** $\frac{3z}{7}$ **e** $\frac{7d}{10}$
   f $\frac{9n}{2}$ **g** $\frac{7a}{3}$ **h** $\frac{5a}{4}$ **i** $\frac{m}{9}$

Page 17 Brackets

1 **a** $2x + 2$ **b** $5y - 15$ **c** $3n + 6$ **d** $8a - 8b$
   e $-4c - 4$ **f** $6x + 30$ **g** $-3z - 12$
   h $10w - 10$ **i** $-2t + 2$
2 **a** $3a + 5$ **b** $3n - 6$ **c** $12 - 5p$ **d** $8 - 2z$
   e $y + 6$ **f** $8s - 13$ **g** $b^2 - 4b$ **h** $2ab - a$
3 **a** $x^2 + 4x + 3$ **b** $x^2 + 7x + 10$
   c $x^2 + 2x - 8$ **d** $x^2 - 1$ **e** $x^2 + 4x + 4$
   f $x^2 + 10x + 25$

Page 17 Equations

1 **a** $x = 2$ **b** $x = 10$ **c** $p = 3$ **d** $m = 4$ **e** $p = 33$
   f $x = 9$ **g** $y = 9$ **h** $c = 7$ **i** $y = 4$ **j** $a = 16$
2 **a** $x = 2$ **b** $x = 4$ **c** $x = 4$ **d** $x = 5$ **e** $x = 10$
   f $x = 2$ **g** $x = 9$ **h** $x = 5$ **i** $x = 8$ **j** $x = 3$
3 **a** $x = 3$ **b** $x = 7$ **c** $x = 11$ **d** $x = 2$ **e** $x = 4$
   f $x = 5$ **g** $x = 4$ **h** $x = 5$ **i** $x = 2$ **j** $x = 6$
4 **a** $x = 2$ **b** $x = 9$ **c** $x = 4$ **d** $x = 3$ **e** $x = 11$
   f $x = 5$ **g** $x = 0$ **h** $x = 1$ **i** $x = 4$ **j** $x = 2$
5 **a** $6(x + 1)$ metres **b** $x = 6$

Page 18 Formulae & substitution

1 **a** 19 **b** 51 **c** 38 **d** 29 **e** 68 **f** 66 **g** 30
   h 19 **i** 49
2 **a** 32 km **b** 8 km **c** 2.4 km **d** 16 km
   e 1.28 km **f** 3.6 km
3 **a** $C = 22h$ **b** £110 **c** £154
4 **a** 60 mph **b** $S = \frac{D}{T}$ **c** $S = 25$ mph
   d 8.9 m/s
5 **a** 4 **b** 18 **c** 27 **d** 50 **e** 23 **f** 48
6 125 cm^3 **7** 24°C

Page 19 Rearranging formulae

1 $a = P - b - c$
2 $d = \frac{C}{\pi}$ **3** $r = \sqrt{\frac{A}{\pi}}$ **4** $w = \sqrt[3]{V}$
5 **a** $a = 5 - 3b$ **b** $a = \frac{6 - b}{2}$ or $a = 3 - \frac{1}{2}b$
   c $a = b^2$ **d** $a = 2b$ **e** $a = \sqrt{b} - 1$ **f** $a = 5b$

Page 20 Sequences & number patterns

1 **a** 16, 19, 22 **b** 49, 59, 69 **c** 70, 65, 60
   d 27, 32, 37 **e** 12, 10, 8 **f** 26, 29, 32

2 **a** Start with 2 squares and add 2 squares
   b $2n$
3 **a** Start with 4 matches and add 3 matches
   b $1 + 3n$
4 **a** 10, 20, 30, 40, 50 **b** 3, 5, 7, 9, 11
   c 3, 7, 11, 15, 19 **d** 7, 10, 13, 16, 19
   e 19, 18, 17, 16, 15 **f** 3, 8, 13, 18, 23
5 **a** 98 **b** 70 **c** 40
6 **a** $2n$ **b** $5n$ **c** $n + 7$ **d** $n + 100$
   e $2n + 1$ **f** $2n - 1$
7 **a** 250, 360, 490 **b** 24, 35, 48
   c 27, 38, 51 **d** 29, 40, 53
8 **a** 6, 9, 14, 21, 30 **b** 3, 12, 27, 48, 75
   c −1, 2, 7, 14, 23
9 **a** $10n^2$ **b** $n^2 - 1$ **c** $n^2 + 2$ **d** $n^2 + 4$

Page 21 Functions & mappings

1 **a** 5, 8, 11, $3x + 2$ **b** 18, 21, 24, $3(x + 5)$
2 2, 5, 10
3

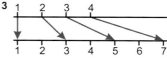

4 $x \to 2x - 1$
5 **a** $x \to x - 3$
   b

6 **a** $x \to \frac{1}{2}x$ **b** $x \to \frac{x + 5}{4}$ **c** $x \to \frac{1}{3}x - 1$

Page 22 Coordinates

1 **a** A(−2, 2), D(−3, −2)
   b

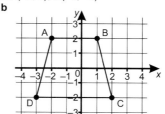

   c Isosceles trapezium
2 A(2, 4), B(5, 0), C(6, 8), D(0, 1),
   E(−8, 0), F(−4, 2), G(0, −3), H(−6, −2),
   I(2, −8), J(−4, −6)

Speedy Revision

Answers

Page 23 Straight-line graphs

1 a

x	−3	−2	−1	0	1	2
y = 2x + 3	−3	−1	1	3	5	7

b

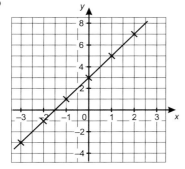

2 **a** 3 **b** −1 **c** 2
3 Yes, because 4 × 7 = 28.
4 **a** y = 4 **b** x = 4 **c** y = −x **d** y = x
5 **c**
6 y = 3x − 1
7 No, they have different gradients (3 and 4).
8 The line goes through (−3, −1) and (0, 2):

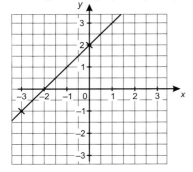

Page 25 Real-life graphs

1 a

Amount in £	0	10	20	30	40	50
Amount in €	0	14	28	42	56	70

b

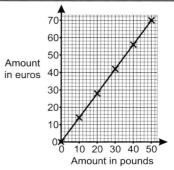

2 **A** Jenny leaves home at 09:00 and cycles to the shop. The shop is 3 miles away, and it takes her 10 minutes.
B Jenny stays at the shop for 10 minutes.
C Jenny is cycling home.
D After 10 minutes she meets her sister, Susie. She walks the remaining 0.4 miles with Susie. Jenny arrives home at 09:40.

Page 26 Inequalities

1 −2, −1, 0, 1, 2, 3, 4, 5
2 40 ⩽ x < 100
3 **a** 1 < x ⩽ 4 **b** x > −3
4

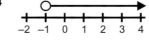

5 a

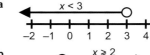

b

c

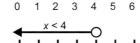

Page 26 Trial & improvement

1 x = 2.7   **2** x = 3.6

Page 27 Units of measurement

1 **a** 1000 cm **b** 100 mm **c** 100 000 m
    d 10 000 g **e** 100 000 ml
2 **a** 12 inches **b** 3 feet
    c 16 ounces **d** 8 pints

Answers

Page 27 Units of measurement (cont)

3 a 30 cm b 1.6 km c 450 g d 30 g
   e 2 pints
4 a 300 cm b 400 cm c 1200 cm
   d 2300 cm e 1960 cm f 75 cm
5 a 20 mm b 50 mm c 110 mm
   d 305 mm e 767 mm f 4 mm
6 a 3000 m b 4000 m c 10 000 m
   d 23 400 m e 50 250 m f 843.5 m
7 a 2000 g b 5000 g c 15 000 g
   d 3500 ml e 9850 ml f 18 635 ml
8 a 20 cm b 3 km c 8 m d 5 litres
   e 7 kg f 14 litres
9 a 4.5 cm b 0.4 kg c 6.75 litres d 62 mm
   e 154 cm f 535 m

Page 28 Reading scales & accuracy

1 a 35 b 28 c 70 d 140 e 37 km/h f 7.8°C
2 $3.5 \leqslant \text{length (m)} < 4.5$ 3 5.5 kg
4 a 10.5 cm, 11.5 cm b 19.5 km, 20.5 km
   c 62.5 kg, 63.5 kg d 99.5 litres, 100.5 litres
   e 18.5 m, 19.5 m f 5.35 cm, 5.45 cm

Page 29 Estimating & measuring angles

1 a 90° b 180° c 270° d 360°
2 a i Between 100° and 110° ii 105°
   b i Between 25° and 35° ii 30°
   c i Between 130° and 140° ii 135°
   d i Between 320° and 340° ii 327°

Page 29 Angles & parallel lines

1 a Obtuse angle
   b Acute angle
   c Right angle
   d Reflex angle
2 a 180° b 360°
   c Vertically opposite
3 a 145° b 26° c 115°
   d 92° e 60°
   f $h = 55°$, $i = 125°$
4

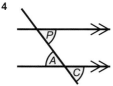

5 a 124° b 118°
   c $x = 78°$, $w = 78°$
   d $y = 76°$, $z = 82°$

Page 31 Polygons

1 a 180° b 360°
2 a 40° b 27° c $x = 95°$, $y = 148°$ d $z = 60°$
3 a 90° b 92° c 92° d 210°
4 a 360° b (number of sides − 2) × 180°
5 a 6 b 120° c 60°

Page 32 Symmetry & properties of shapes

1 a   b

   c   d

2 a i 3 ii 3
   b i 0 ii 2
   c i 2 ii 2
   d i 4 ii 4
3 a A, E, H, M, T, U, W b H, N, S, Z c F, P
4 a 4 b 4
5 Slice vertically through the vertex at the top and a diameter of the base.
6 a Kite
   b Trapezium
   c Parallelogram
7

Name of polygon	Number of sides	All sides equal?	All angles equal?	Number of lines of symmetry	Order of rotation symmetry
Square	4	Yes	Yes	4	4
Rectangle	4	No	Yes	2	2
Isosceles triangle	3	No	No	1	1
Equilateral triangle	3	Yes	Yes	3	3
Rhombus	4	Yes	No	2	2
Kite	4	No	No	1	1
Trapezium	4	No	No	0	1
Regular pentagon	5	Yes	Yes	5	5
Parallelogram	4	No	No	0	2

Speedy Revision

Answers

Page 34 Reflection

1 a 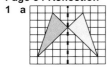 **b**

c **d**

2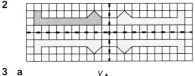

3 a

b $y = -1$

Page 35 Rotation

1 a 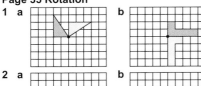 **b**

2 a **b**

3 a 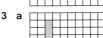 **b**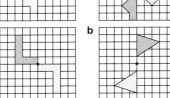

4 a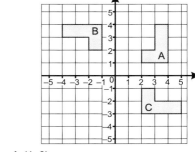

b (1, 0)

Page 36 Translation

1 a **b**

2 a 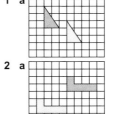 **b**

3 a **b**

4 a 6 right, 1 down **b** 5 right, 1 up
  c 1 right, 5 down **d** 5 left, 5 down
  e 8 left, 4 up **f** 4 right, 1 up
  g 1 left, 5 down **h** 12 right, 1 up

Page 37 Enlargement

1 a 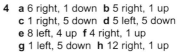 **b**

c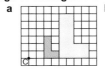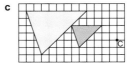

Answers

Page 37 Enlargement (cont)

2 **a** **b**

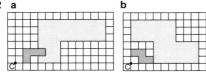

c

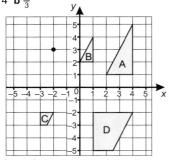

3 **a** 4 **b** $\frac{1}{3}$

4 **a**

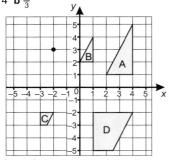

b Scale factor 3, centre (–5, –2)

Page 38 Perimeter & circumference

1 **a** 14 cm **b** 13.4 m
2 **a** 32 cm **b** 40 cm **c** 30 cm **d** 25.6 cm
3 **a** 18.8 cm **b** 29.5 cm **c** 25.1 cm
4 **a** 12.9 cm **b** 21.7 cm

Page 39 Areas of triangles & quadrilaterals

1 **a** Area = $\frac{1}{2}$ × base × height
   b Area = base × perpendicular height
   c Area = $\frac{1}{2}$ × sum of parallel sides × height
2 **a** 10 cm² **b** 5 cm² **c** 18 cm² **d** 10.5 m²
3 **a** 8 cm² **b** 15 cm²
4 **a** 10 cm² **b** 18 cm²
5 **a** 6 m² **b** 17 m² **c** 705.5 mm² **d** 11.28 cm²

Page 40 Areas of circles & composite shapes

1 **a** 78.5 cm² **b** 153.9 cm² **c** 25.5 m²
2 **a** 9.82 cm² **b** 29.1 cm² **c** 25.8 cm²
   d 33.62 cm²

Page 40 More circles

1 **a** i 6.28 cm **ii** 12.6 cm²
   b i 7.30 m **ii** 11.3 m²
   c i 31.8 cm **ii** 128.8 cm²   **2** 142°

Page 41 Pythagoras' theorem

1 **a** 13 cm **b** 53 m **c** 7.2 cm **d** 24.2 m
   e 4.3 m **f** 8.5 cm
2 **a** 8 cm **b** 16 cm **c** 9.1 m **d** 7.3 m
   e 6.5 cm **f** 9.9 cm
3 7.6 km   **4** 3.4 m
5 **a** 5 units **b** 25 units **c** 29 units
   d 4.5 units **e** 13 units **f** 10.3 units

Page 42 Nets & 3-D shapes; plans & elevations

1 **a** and **c**
2 **a** Triangular prism
   b Regular tetrahedron
   c Square-based pyramid
3 **a** **b**

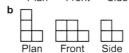

c

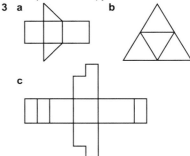

4 **a**

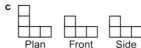

Plan   Front   Side

b

Plan   Front   Side

c

Plan   Front   Side

d

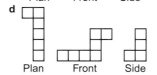

Plan   Front   Side

5 **a**

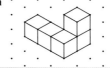

Answers

Page 42 Nets & 3-D shapes; plans & elevations (cont)

b

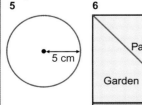

Page 43 Volume & surface area

1 a 6.776 cm³ b 9.802 m³ c 2420.88 cm³
d 30.69 m³
2 a i 4 cm² ii 28 cm³ b i 21 m² ii 210 m³
3 216 m³
4 a 42.4 m³ b 384.1 m³
5 a 24 cm² b 22 cm² c 14 cm²
6 a 22 cm² b 33.54 m² c 70.7 m²
d 520 m² e 314 m²
7 4 m 8 3.8 m
9 a 40 000 cm² b 100 000 cm² c 5000 cm²
10 a 0.3 m² b 2 m² c 0.01 m²
11 a 4 000 000 cm³ b 25 000 000 cm³
c 20 000 cm³
12 a 7 m³ b 75 m³ c 0.04 m³

Page 45 Bearings & scale drawings

1 a 050° b 305°
2 a 150 km b 250 km c 12.5 km
3 a 2 cm b 0.5 cm c 0.4 mm
4 a 130° b 040° c 220° d 8 km
e 17 km f 15 km

Page 46 Compound measures

1 a 57.5 km/h b 85 km/h c 72 km/h
d 90 km/h
2 a 135 miles b 9 miles c 7 hours
d 1 hour 20 minutes
3 a 54 g b 2 700 000 g or 2700 kg
c 30 cm³ d 370 cm³

Page 46 Constructions & loci

5 6

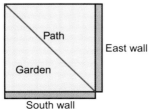

7

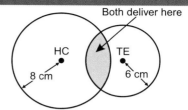

Both deliver here

HC   TE

8 cm   6 cm

Page 48 Mean, median, mode, range

1 C
2 a 31 days b 2 hours
3 a 2, 4, 4, 5, 6, 7, 8; median = 5 pens
b 1, 2, 4, 4, 5, 6, 7, 7; median = 4.5 hours
4 a 22.2 cars b £6
5 a 10 b 230 ants c 10 kg
6 a Mean = 3.5 m, median = 3 m,
mode = 3 m and 4 m, range = 4 m
b Mean = 14.77 ml, median = 13.15 ml,
mode = 12.3 ml, range = 8.6 ml
c Mean = 18 carrots, median = 17 carrots,
mode = 23 carrots, range = 26 carrots
d Mean = 66.5 kg, median = 66.8 kg,
no mode, range = 6.6 kg
7 $1\frac{1}{3}$ cars
8 Although Jerome gets more text
messages on average, the range shows
that some days he gets none at all. Kay's
range shows that she had at least one
text message every day last month, so
she is more likely to get one today.

Page 49 Collecting data & two-way tables

1 a Question 1: The options are too vague:
'occasionally' could mean different things
to different people. Jenny should give
definite options such as 'less than once
a month', 'at least once a month but not
every week', 'every week'.
Question 2: Leading question: never start
a question 'Do you agree...'
Question 3: Too personal and not really
relevant.
b At that time, people who go to work or
school will not be surveyed.
People outside the swimming pool are
likely to like the swimming pool, so Jenny
will miss people who do not like it.
2 Primary data is data you collect yourself.
Secondary data is data that other people
have collected.

Answers

Page 49 Collecting data & two-way tables (cont)

3 **a**, **b**, **d** Continuous **c** Discrete

4

	MP3	MP4	Total
Boys own	15	6	21
Girls own	17	3	20
Total	32	9	41

5

	Red	Blue	Silver	Total
Trek	3	4	2	9
Giant	5	6	4	15
Total	8	10	6	24

Page 50 Frequency tables

1

Colour of book	Tally	Frequency
Yellow	JHT	5
Orange	JHT	5
Purple	JHT JHT	10
	Total	20

2 a

No. of potatoes	Tally	Frequency
26 to 35	JHT II	7
36 to 45	JHT III	8
46 to 55	JHT	5
	Total	20

b

No. of potatoes	Tally	Frequency
$20 \leqslant N < 30$	III	3
$30 \leqslant N < 40$	JHT II	7
$40 \leqslant N < 50$	JHT II	7
$50 \leqslant N < 60$	III	3
	Total	20

3

Test score	Tally	Frequency
$0 \leqslant S < 10$	II	2
$10 \leqslant S < 20$	III	3
$20 \leqslant S < 30$	IIII	4
$30 \leqslant S < 40$	IIII	4
$40 \leqslant S < 50$	II	2
$50 \leqslant S < 60$	II	2
	Total	17

4 **a** 16.6 kg **b** $12 \leqslant W < 18$ **c** $18 \leqslant W < 24$

Page 51 Bar charts & frequency diagrams

1 5 + 4 + 7 = 16 medals

2

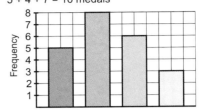

3

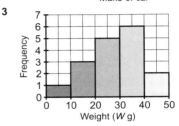

4

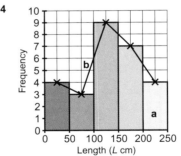

5

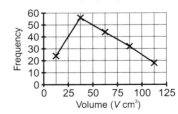

Speedy Revision